Wilhelm Rein, Charles Cecil Van Liew

Outlines of Pedagogics

Wilhelm Rein, Charles Cecil Van Liew

Outlines of Pedagogics

ISBN/EAN: 9783743338692

Manufactured in Europe, USA, Canada, Australia, Japa

Cover: Foto ©Thomas Meinert / pixelio.de

Manufactured and distributed by brebook publishing software (www.brebook.com)

Wilhelm Rein, Charles Cecil Van Liew

Outlines of Pedagogics

" Ich glaube nicht, dass ich viel eignes neues lehre,
Noch durch mein Scherflein Witz den Schatz der Weisheit mehre.
Doch denk' ich von der Müh mir zweierlei Gewinn;
Einmal, dass ich nun selbst an Einsicht weiter bin;
Sodann, dass doch dadurch an manchen Mann wird kommen
Manches, wovon er sonst gar hätte nichts vernommen,
Und auch der dritte Grund scheint wert nicht des Gelächters:
Das, wer dies Büchlein liest, derweil doch liest kein schlechters."

RÜCKERT
(Weisheit der Brahmanen).

OUTLINES OF PEDAGOGICS

BY

PROFESSOR W. REIN

DIRECTOR OF THE PEDAGOGICAL SEMINARY AT THE UNIVERSITY OF JENA

TRANSLATED BY

C. C. AND IDA J. VAN LIEW

WITH ADDITIONAL NOTES BY THE FORMER

LONDON
SWAN SONNENSCHEIN & CO.
SYRACUSE, N.Y.: C. W. BARDEEN
1893

TRANSLATORS' PREFACE.

NEVER in the history of education have the educational forces of the world been more on the alert, more inspired with the desire to advance professionally, than to-day. At a time when all society is affected by the progressive and investigative spirit of the age, when sociological and political problems are being viewed in a new, often revolutionary, light, when all classes are becoming interested not merely in the welfare, the preservation of self, but also in the welfare of *all* humanity, and when, at the same time, certain powerful tendencies are constantly appearing that seem to endanger society, it behoves the educator not only to be progressive, but to ask himself whether his work is placing that stamp upon humanity which will make human individuals *trustworthy* reformers, leaders, thinkers, voters. He has been busy during the last century in raising the intellectual standard of all classes, in placing knowledge and power in the hands of the low as well as the high ; it now belongs to his office to reflect as to what kind of weapons this knowledge and this power are to become. To-day, therefore, we find educators turning more and more to the conception that education, both as a social and a national factor, must, above all, construct character; its various aims and the forces it applies to accomplish them must concentrate in character-building. In this tendency we may find a partial explanation of the great power which the Herbartian school of pedagogics possesses in Germany, and the attention which it is rapidly attracting in other countries. In fact, the Herbartian system, in its truest significance, cannot be regarded as an arbitrary, subjective creation, but as the outcome of an historical development, reinforced by the results of philosophic and scientific research. We are occasionally told to-day that we should avoid everything in education that smacks of a "system." This conception rests upon the false assumption that system is avoidable, a premise that we can by no means grant. Every educational institution is, and must be, the living exemplification of some more or less clearly-defined and well-founded system. It is not a question of "system or no system," but of whether the system shall be clearly defined, firmly established, and harmoniously articulated, or indefinite, faulty, and hence inefficient. It is a question of whether the educator shall be but dimly conscious of the aim of his work and the means for its attainment, or whether his efforts shall be reinforced and the fruits of his labour increased and insured by a system of clear, definite, guiding conceptions that constitute an organic whole. Students of pedagogy in the past have been inclined to content themselves with a study of pedagogical arts, manners, and devices (the external aids of instruction), and to neglect the fundamental conceptions that lend inner harmony to education. System and organization, however, by no means exclude progress and new light. No one who has made himself thoroughly acquainted with the history of the Herbartian school can ascribe to it either exclusivism or lack of a progressive and scientific spirit. In fact, common grounds, in the midst of minor differences of opinion, have insured it a rapid progress and an unusually prominent and influential position among modern educational movements.

Modern research in the field of the history of education is characterized by two tendencies—the one seeks to profit by the history of past experience and efforts, the other to learn from the present achievements of the educational *world*. No country has attracted a more universal attention, educationally, than Germany. As Compagré says: "For two centuries Germany has been the classical land of pedagogy." But it is not that which is specifically German that attracts; the educational world does not desire to be Germanized, but to lay claim to the general truths that the history of German pedagogics presents in the work of such educational reformers as Comenius, Basedow, Ratich, Pestalozzi, Froebel, and Herbart. No more fruitful or influential work has been accomplished in pedagogics than that of Herbart and the Herbartian school.

It is the aim of this work to furnish a brief introduction to the Herbartian pedagogics, upon whose principles it is based. It presents the author's views as to their modern application. Hence, it is well fitted to serve as an introduction to the study of Herbart and his school. Every thorough student of pedagogics, it is true, must ultimately refer to the prime fountain—the works of Herbart himself; he must become his own interpreter of the philosopher's words. But he cannot afford to neglect the results that over fifty years of development since Herbart's death have produced.

The second edition of Professor Rein's *Pädagogik im Grundriss* (Sammlung Göschen, Stuttgart, 1893), contained some essential additions and changes; on this account certain parts of the first edition, referring chiefly to Part I., were omitted to make room for the new. Since these omissions affected much interesting material, all that both editions contain has been combined in the translation.

The chapters upon the kinds of schools and school administration refer directly to the German school system, it is true; but the problems discussed are of universal interest. At present the relative interests and rights of State, Church, community and family in education, the relative value and the organization of classical and scientific courses, the classification and administration of schools, and the training of teachers, are all subjects of earnest discussion among the educational circles of almost every civilized land. The views of the author differ in some respects from existing practices, but his classification of schools is based upon the present system, and the particulars in which he differs from it have been indicated. These chapters, therefore, will serve, as an additional subordinate aim, to give the reader an insight into the German school system, which is so much discussed to-day, and into certain lines of proposed reform. Here a few brief paragraphs have been added for the purpose of facilitating a comparison with English and American schools.

The chapters upon the succession, co-ordination (the curriculum), and treatment of the material of instruction have also been enlarged for the purpose of *illustrating* the *general* application of the principles they present. The bibliographies have been retained as in the original, and an attempt has been made to furnish a list of the English literature that has thus far appeared upon the Herbartian pedagogics.

JENA, *January*, 1893.   V. L.

AUTHOR'S PREFACE.

THE question as to the best form or the most complete system of education is obviously one of the deepest and most impressive problems that engages the attention of everyone that stands in the midst of the activity of public life—the statesman and the friend of the people, as well as the solitary thinker. The most manifold lines of human reflection, and the most diverse motives of human action, centre in education. None other than such questions as: What is human happiness?—and, How may the rising generation be led to this highest aim?—What efforts must society make in order to approach nearer to its destiny? show the significance and difficulty of this problem, which, in its social phases, is closely connected with all social problems.

He who is accustomed not to content himself with the surface, but to get at the bottom of a question, would at first be dismayed at the mass of relations that focus, as it were, at this point. At the same time, however, he would soon feel the necessity of finding his way out of the mass, and, above all, of throwing light upon the question as to what education aims at and is able to do.

This need can only be satisfied by preparing a systematically arranged whole that is characterized by carefully developed conceptions, and suited by virtue of its clearness to supply a firm foundation upon which the foot may rest tranquilly in the midst of contradictory opinions.

But, of course, a system is of value only to him in whom it has developed. The truth that has *merely* been learned adheres to us like a false member, a false tooth, or a waxen nose. The system that has *merely* been learned has no power, and acquires no significance, for the mental life. It is a lifeless fund from which streams no animating warmth, no life-giving energy, Only the truth that has been obtained by one's own reflection resembles the natural member; it alone really belongs to us; it penetrates our entire being, elevates us, affords us certainty, insures us the full power of conviction, and gives impulse to a manifold activity.

Nevertheless, I undertake to present in this work the outlines of a system of pedagogics. Not everyone can beget each thought anew in himself. Otherwise, why the collection and transmission of already acquired intellectual treasures? But everyone should seek to enter thoroughly and heartily into that which the labour of another has produced; he should test for himself in how far it can lay claim to truth, and assist him in his own search for clear, stable convictions.

In view of the brevity imposed upon the series of publications[1] among which this work appears, nothing more than an introductory survey of the broad field of education and educational work can be given. Such a comprehensive survey is necessary for all those who have the education of the people at heart, especially for those to whom both the supervision and education of the rising generation in the lower, middle, and higher schools is entrusted.

With the above end in view, I present this volume. May it not appear unworthy to the pedagogical interest which prevails in our age; may it inspire to new reflections, and help to level the way for a rational education among the people.

W. REIN.

JENA, 10th August, 1892.

---

[1] Sammlung Göschen.

TABLE OF CONTENTS.

	PAGE
TRANSLATORS' PREFACE	v
AUTHOR'S PREFACE	ix
INTRODUCTION	1
PART I.—*Practical Pedagogics*	12
(*A*) OF THE FORMS OF EDUCATION	15
1. Home Education	15
2. Education in Private Boarding Schools, etc.	19
3. Of School Education	23
(*a*) The People's School	30
(*b*) The Real-Schools	35
(*c*) The Gymnasium	37
(*d*) The Schools for Girls	45
(*B*) OF SCHOOL ADMINISTRATION	49
1. School Legislation	49
2. School Equipment	57
3. School Supervision	59
4. Preparation and Training of Teachers	61
PART II.—*Theoretical Pedagogics*	65
(*A*) OF THE AIM OF EDUCATION—TELEOLOGY	66
1. Conception of Education	66
2. Plurality of Educational Purposes	69
3. The Uniform Purpose	70

(B) OF THE MEANS OF EDUCATION—METHODOLOGY	78
1. THEORY OF INSTRUCTION	86
I. General Didactics	86
1. The General Aim of Instruction	86
2. The Means of Instruction	93
(a) Selection of the Material for Instruction	93
(b) Co-ordination Do. Do.	101
[Supplementary Remarks upon the Application of the Historical Stages of Culture and Concentration]	116
(c) Treatment of the Material for Instruction	135
[Supplementary Remarks upon the Application of the Formal Steps]	146
II. Special Didactics	158
2. THEORY OF GUIDANCE	163
I. Training	163
II. Government of Children	178
III. Physical Education	182
LITERARY REFERENCES	185

OUTLINES OF PEDAGOGICS.

INTRODUCTION.

ACCORDING to Kant, the great secret of the perfection of human nature lies concealed in education. It is delightful to imagine that human nature will always be developed to something higher and better by education, and that the latter may be brought into a form suited to mankind. In such meditations we picture to ourselves a future happier humanity. How gladly would we dwell upon this thought that once inspired Plato to exclaim: "There is nothing more divine than education." Without this feeling of inspiration, without such a lofty purpose ever before the eyes, educators would hardly be able persistently to endure the constant sacrifice that they make in forcing themselves to bend the virile intellect to the child's world. They would hardly be able to overcome the conception that the world will remain as it is in spite of education, if they were not always animated by the hope that their efforts would bear rich fruits in the individual and in society.

It is the thought of ennobling the human race

which, ever and again, engages the attention of both the educators and the friends of the people.

Eloquent words often portray for us how vain it is to hope for better *times* if *man* himself is not bettered. The cultivation of humanity must begin within man himself and radiate from him to society. What is gained if we succeed in advancing the cultivation of the soil, in enlivening the commercial and industrial spirit everywhere, in giving the greatest degree of perfection to the laws and statutes of countries, when man himself is not worthy of inhabiting such a beautiful earth, is not able to find a heaven in it?

In fact the idea is often directly expressed, that the destiny of a nation, its prime as well as its decay, depends almost entirely upon the education that falls to the lot of its youth. Friedrich the Great also did reverence to this thought in the words: "He who considers mankind good, does not understand the human race; for mankind left to himself is brutal. Only education is able to ennoble him." The same conception is also emphasized by the philosopher of Königsberg [1] in the following proposition: "Man can only become human through education. He is nothing except what education makes of him."

In view of such opinions it seems to be easily conceivable that new efforts are constantly being made to clarify, explain, and arrange the manifold views as to the purpose, means, and methods of education, and to condense them into a form which, in accordance with the saying of the above-mentioned sage, is suited to mankind. It is explicable why one is never tired of proclaiming that that people is mightiest and happi-

---

[1] Kant.— *T's.*

est which, in accordance with this form of education, has attained the deepest and broadest culture, extending even to the lowest strata of society; that it is invincible by its neighbours, and either envied by its contemporaries or regarded as an illustrious example for their imitation.

And we certainly do not reason thus unjustly; for the historical power of education asserts itself very perceptibly whenever new thoughts are to be infused into the life and character of a new generation.

Hence, one might easily be tempted to overrate the power of education when he sees that the most distinguished intellects expect everything of it. But the facts of everyday life admonish us to be discreet. Do we not constantly see both children and nations that fall far short of the ideal which educators have sketched for them, and again, others without special preparation who, following solely their own inward impulse, and even under the most adverse external circumstances, advance nobly and raise themselves far above the stratum from which they started? In some cases, therefore, we meet with retrogression in defiance of all education, in others, progress by virtue of self-power. But what becomes of the improvement of *all* humanity, what of that enchanting vision of the human race made happier by an education that is arranged with a definite aim?

It would obviously be quite wrong to attempt to question the power of education in general because it has not always achieved either in individuals or in entire generations that which it had in view. Without doubt Nature and the world do much more for those who are to be educated than education itself, as a rule, can boast of accomplishing. But on the other hand it cannot be disputed that those evil influences in Nature and the world which also assail the educable individual, may likewise be met effectively by a systematically arranged education. And this view is also deeply rooted in the common consciousness of society. Would the family and society otherwise devote such profound interest and such constant care and encouragement to an institution of whose inefficiency everyone was sufficiently convinced? How often one hears the complaint among the events of everyday life that the wreck of some young human being is the consequence of a wrong or deficient education!

How often very conspicuous deficiencies are excused by the faulty method of education! On the contrary, also, we often meet with the expression of pessimistic views which agree with the words of Horace, "Naturam expellas furca, tamen usque recurret"—"Though you drive out Nature with a pitchfork, yet will she always return."

Opinions vacillate between these two extremes. At one time all results are ascribed to necessity, Nature, or heredity; at another to freedom, art, or individual acquisition. Society, not to be misled by this strife, takes its stand in favour of education, for it will not leave the development of the rising generation to chance. Hence it has organized a great variety of institutions and schools in which to prepare its youth for the various positions and tasks of life.

If the families, above all, care for the education of the single individual, the schools on their part should preserve and impart the inherited blessings of civilization, those priceless treasures upon which thousands of years have laboured. They should strive to develop efficient members of society, that the people may never be lacking in national power, nor the Church in worshippers of the Divine. This position of the schools among human institutions is based upon the conception of a gradual moral inspiration of society as the highest stage of moral development which it must strive to attain.

Upon this highest stage of development the community would appear as truly morally inspired. All society is, then, pervaded by a clear insight into the ethical ideas which govern the entire social body, and inspired by a firm will to obey this insight, to present a symmetrical and, as far as possible, complete embodiment of the moral ideas, as the loftiest mission of life. In order gradually to approach this ideal of a morally inspired community, various institutions are necessary. The indispensable foundation of all moral progress is a thorough, firmly established, legal order. Without this society becomes alarmed and disordered, and either labours but little or not at all. The interdependence of the various activities of life, the fitting division of labour is effected only upon a strictly legal basis. At first, therefore, society exists in the form of a legal community for the purpose of bringing about the complete realization of the idea of rights within the entire body. In conjunction with a well-perfected system of rewards and punishments, it aims to remove from social life, as far as possible, those elements that are repugnant to human nature—strife and the infringement of personal rights; and to leave no evil deeds unpunished nor good deeds unrewarded. Proceeding upon this foundation, the administrative system can undertake to provide abundantly for the material wants in order to engender that social disposition which is necessary for all scientific and artistic production, and to place at disposal the means by which various institutions may be maintained. The establishment and care of the latter is the task of the educational system, which could not exist without the above-mentioned social regulations, but which on the other hand pays society a liberal interest upon all that it has received from them. In that it generally nourishes a sturdy sense of law, order, and justice, and cultivates the sense of right, it raises the mere legal community up to a higher plane upon which strife, infringement of rights and deeds of rough violence are abominated. The influence of culture shows itself to be just as beneficent in its effects upon the system of rewards and punishments, for a higher culture ennobles and refines the reward, and tempers the punishments. It also affects the administrative system by awakening an insight into the beauty of benevolence, and thereby gradually developing the public sympathy for the mutual interests of society, and a readiness to make sacrifice on their behalf; it stamps upon all a conviction that every thorough and lasting reform in social life is to be sought only in the constant, systematic elevation of the national culture. Only from this starting-point can the highest form of social life, the permanent moral inspiration of society, be gradually approached.

Such a systematic and well-planned education of both the individual and the entire social body becomes so much the more necessary in proportion as those influences are stronger which, as the occult coadjutors of education, might endanger its success.

Both the circle of the family and that of social intercourse are subjected to forces that are active in the entire social body, and that penetrate the entire atmosphere of human life in invisible channels. No one knows whence these currents, these ideas arise; but they are there. They influence the moods, the aspirations, and the inclinations of humanity, and no one however powerful can withdraw himself from their effects; no sovereign's command makes its way into their depths. They are often born of a genius to be seized upon by the multitude that soon forgets their author; then the power of the thought that has thus become active in the masses again impels the individual to energetic resolutions: in this manner it is constantly describing a remarkable circle. Originating with those that are highly gifted, these thoughts permeate all society, reaching, in fact, not only its adult members, but also through these its youth, and appearing again in other highly gifted individuals in whom they will perhaps have been elevated to a definite form.

Whether the power of these dominant ideas is greater in the individual, or in the body of individuals as a whole, is a matter of indifference here. Be that as it may, it cannot be denied that their effect upon the one is manifested in a reciprocal action upon the other, and that their influence upon the younger generation is indisputable. When the older generation has lost its moral elasticity, it will not seem astonishing if the succeeding generation seeks to surpass its ancestors in sensuality and in the race after material possessions. Both the spirit of the family and the spirit of society, working together either in harmony or in strife, act uninterruptedly upon the formation of the youthful minds, and influence them either for evil or for good.

Besides these factors, two especial institutions, both of which are strong and accustomed to rule, seek to obtain possession of the youth. Both endeavour to test their strength for the purpose of determining in how far they can draw the educational establishments of the people into their power. These two institutions are the Church and the State. The former desires to educate faithful members, the latter obedient citizens. Since something always depends upon the foundation that is laid, each desires to direct the education of the youth conformably to its own judgment, in accordance with the well-known maxim: "He who has the youth has the future."

In either case education will receive a very definite and fixed stamp. At one time we shall hear of the State system of pedagogy, at another time of the Church system of pedagogy. Each will have its various shades according to the different conceptions and the different constitutions of the State or the Church. For example, in the past, education by the State has received special forms in the organization of the ancient State, or in certain philosophical systems, such as that of Plato or Fichte. Education by the Church has received a very marked character in the pedagogics of the Jesuits.

Of all powers that would take possession of education, State and Church are the most influential. But if we review once more the series of educational forces—Nature, family, social intercourse, the tendencies manifested in the spirit of the times, the political and ecclesiastical constitution of society—we shall find that they affect education in part occultly and without being conscious of the end in view, in part in a designedly systematic way. To the occult coadjutors of education belong without doubt the tendencies manifested in the spirit of the age, social intercourse, and Nature. The education of the youth will be controlled in a designedly systematic manner by the family, the Church, and the State. Each one of these will exercise a determinative influence; each will endeavour to mould the rising youth according to its own views. No prudent and intelligent person would dispute the right of the family to do this; but this natural right is too often curtailed by the claims which State and Church advance. How often these two powers are at variance with one another, each endeavouring to gain the advantage over the other! Hence, from this point of view also, the great significance of education in the life of nations becomes clearly apparent. The reflective man finds it easy to explain why the friends of the people, in proportion as they strive more faithfully for intellectual and moral elevation, endeavour to penetrate more and more deeply and permanently into the great questions of education in all its phases—the ethical, the psychological, and the sociological. Their eyes should be open to both the occult and the visible influences to which the growing youth are exposed. They are, therefore, forced to consider the question: Is there a higher unity which possesses the power to remove the opposing influences and to unite and blend the good forces with itself?

Will it be possible to find a form of education which, in accordance with the words of Kant, is suited to the needs of humanity? Shall we ever succeed in establishing an educational system which contains no contradiction within itself, is pervaded by an harmonious spirit, and is able to attract and fill with a lasting inspiration the good and noble men of all nations?

Such is our hope, and such are our endeavours at least; for the thought as to what would become of the rising generation if left alone at the mercy of those powers, is too distressing. Would not this be leaving education to chance,—which were no wiser than writing letters in the sand of the sea-shore? If we desire at all to lead the rising generation to a higher stage of development, a direct, systematic, conscious influence, such as can only result from a well-pondered and firmly-established system of education, must be placed over against the invisible, unconscious, but ever active influences.

The vast extent of this theme requires at first a clear preparatory survey. Two fields of investigation may be clearly distinguished within the entire sphere of pedagogy.

1. The investigations are directed first to the actual relations of life, to the arrangements for public and private education, and the present usage as it has developed in the course of centuries. We here enter the sphere of practical pedagogics. To this subject belong the questions of school legislation (school administration, school equipment, school organisation, etc.) of domestic and institutional education, and of pedagogics as applied to the gymnasium and to the common people's school.

2. If we inquire into the nature and conception, the necessity and possibility, the limits and aims, and the ways and means of education, our investigations fall under the head of *theoretical* pedagogics.

Both divisions, the theoretical and the practical, together constitute *systematic* pedagogics: beside the latter stands *historical* pedagogics. If we view the present system of education as a development, and investigate the conditions under which this development has taken place, we are occupied with historical pedagogics. It belongs to the province of this department of pedagogics to delineate the educational conditions of the past, and to pursue their development up to the present.

Accordingly we may fix upon the following classification:—

PEDAGOGICS.

(*a*) Systematic Pedagogics.	(*b*) Historical Pedagogics.
I. Practical Pedagogics. II. Theoretical Pedagogics.	

In the following chapters we propose to give a survey of the systematic department of pedagogics, and to this end we shall first enter upon the consideration of practical pedagogics.

PART I.

Practical Pedagogics.

THE philosophical examination of the practical conditions under which education may take place is comprehended under the conception of practical pedagogics. It aims to present and establish those common laws for the conditions of education which belong to a definite class. The process of education is accomplished in certain concrete forms which change according to the standard of the place, time, and persons, and which stand in certain relations to the central points of the external organization of society, to the family, community, State, and Church.

It is the task of practical pedagogics to point out these relations, to indicate the equilibrium of forces which constitute modern society, with reference to the organization of the school system,—in short, to present the various forms of education under which the cultivation of the rising generation is being accomplished, and to reveal their best organization. It aims to survey the entire system and organization of education, to determine the relative position of its single departments, and to set the limits between them according to their purpose and form.

Practical pedagogics surveys the manifold concrete forms of life in the light of certain conceptions; in inquiring into the *place, time,* and *persons* upon which education is encumbent, it arrives at the following aggroupment.

1. Education takes place in the home, in the family. Here it is chiefly the *private* education of the *individual.*

2. Education is also cared for in special private institutions. Here it appears as *private* education in *masses.*

3. Education is undertaken by the public schools, where it appears in the form of *public* education in *masses.*

We meet with education in these three forms; they are to be briefly discussed in the following paragraphs, that we may then consider the subject of school administration in its various departments. The following synopsis indicates the order in which these subjects will be presented.

PRACTICAL PEDAGOGICS.

(A) OF THE FORMS OF EDUCATION.

I. Separate Education of the Individual.
  1. Private. Home Education.
  2. Public.

II. Education *en masse*.
  1. Private. Education in Private Institutions.
  2. Public. Education in Public Schools.

(B) OF SCHOOL ADMINISTRATION.

1. Legislation.
2. Equipment.
3. Supervision.
4. Preparation and Training of Teachers.

(A) OF THE FORMS OF EDUCATION.

1. *Of Home Education.*

"Erziehung ist Sache der Familien; von da geht sie aus und dahin kehrt sie grösstenteils zurück."—*Herbart.*

In the education of the home there is a concentration of all educative activities within the limits of a single circle of life. This circle is the result of a natural union based upon a common parentage, and is therefore contained within narrow bounds. Three factors in particular are of importance in determining its efficiency: (1) The sense of the unity and relationship of all members, which arises from the common parentage. (2) The feeling of dependence upon a head of the family, which is the result of daily observations as to the manner in which all are supported. (3) The very intimate knowledge of the younger members of the family as the result of their gradual growth and the familiar intercourse of the family.

Let us now consider these separate factors somewhat more closely.

1. The chief distinctive characteristic of the family is its unity. Unity and concentration are two of the chief demands that are placed upon education. Hence the family seems to be an especially favourable foothold for education. Above all it is a fact which harmonizes remarkably well with the Germanic sentiment that the family always appears as that

relation which education should desire and further. As long as a nation is ruled by this sentiment it will maintain its own power and health.

The following facts show how favourable a foothold the family provides for education. How speedily willing eyes and ready hands are to be found in the family; how quickly the division of labour is organized here, not for the sake of sordid gain, but because of the silent power of attraction that radiates directly from the neediest members of the circle. Furthermore, how easily the warm atmosphere of the home develops various inclinations and interests, whose transplantation to the school often requires such great exertions. In the family every interest springs up easily and spontaneously. The younger members look to the older; the entire circle observes with interest the first movements of the awakening life, and furthers the first trials from which definite tendencies of the infant soul develop. Also nowhere can so favourable an environment for the development of sympathy and good-will be found as in the family. It is just these first fundamental elements that are of such great consequence in the entire after life. The utmost care is often unable to compensate later in life for that which was neglected in earlier years. The narrow limitation of the family circle, the restriction of the sympathy to its few members, is the most natural preliminary condition for the development of sympathetic interest and good-will. Also the subjective traits of character, introspection, and self-command, will hardly be more sure of advancement than where several persons are constantly associated, where they observe and judge one another with impartiality, and place the common honour in the right relations.

2. The unity of the family is the strongest that could be conceived, because the sense of common parentage, which rests upon physical presuppositions, vouches for the relationship of all members. The blessed effect of this relationship depends above all upon the one weighty supposition that there is a centre for all members of the family from which all chief activities proceed, about which all else circles, and by whose will the entire body is permeated and governed. In these respects the small circle of the family resembles very closely the greater circle of the State, in so far as the latter, also, can not afford to be deprived of the power which binds its members together and which protects each single activity, if it would not be rent asunder. The members of the family look confidently to the head; and this sense of dependence favours, at the same time, the proper reception of that which is dearest to mankind, namely, the religious feeling. If the life of the family is permeated by a noble piety, a sincere religious faith will take root in the hearts of the children. Faithful devotion to the guide of the youth also calls forth faithful devotion to Him who controls human destinies,—a thought which Herbart expresses so beautifully in the words: "To the child, the family should be the symbol of the order in the world; from the parents one should derive by idealization the characteristics of the deity."

3. In the third place, we called attention to the fact that the intercourse of the family results in the most intimate knowledge of its younger members, an ele-

ment that is very essential for education. Accuracy in the comprehension of child-natures is to the educator what knowledge of the soil is to the farmer. This accuracy is secured by extensive intercourse with the child in its earlier years much more easily than later; for the child's nature loses its transparency as its age increases, not because of a presupposed purpose on the part of the child to be reticent and reserved, but because the gradually increasing vigour of inner processes produces a shyness of contact with strangers and the external world, and because it is only upon more intimate intercourse that the boy is inclined to permit this inner life to be scrutinized. The conditions necessary for obtaining a grasp of the inner life of the child are present in the family. Therefore, by way of a brief recapitulation, we may well say that both the care and development of the body, and the formation of the mind and character can thrive nowhere so well as in the domain of home education. The family, as a power upon which the future of a child depends, will always be one of the chief subjects for consideration, both in the inner and outer phases of its life, wherever the problems of education demand attention. Hence, one finds it easy to explain why Pestalozzi conceived the idea of placing the education in the hands of the mothers. We are indebted to him for the imperishable conception that the home education lays the foundation-stone of all human culture, and that the deep impressions which the intimate relations of the family and the order and customs of the home make upon the development of the child, cannot be supplied by any other device. The fatal error in Rousseau's ideas lay in the exclusion of the parents from the education of Emil, and in the attempt to concentrate all the educative power in the teacher. He despaired of being able to establish uniformity and consistency in the plan and organization of education otherwise than by the separation of the family and the school. The knot which Rousseau cut, a more judicious theory of education seeks to untie. The education of the children will always remain the holiest and highest of all family duties. The welfare, civilization, and culture of a people depend essentially upon the degree of success that attends the education in the homes. The family principle is the point at which both the religious and educational life of a people centres, and about which it revolves. It is a force in comparison with which every sovereign's command appears powerless.

2. *Of Education in Certain Institutions that aim to take the place of the Family for the time being.*

The boarding school represents, as it were, an enlarged family. It has, in fact, certain essential characteristics in common with the family, but differs from the latter so greatly that one cannot properly speak of a likeness between such an institution as a boarding school and the family.

The boarding school cannot be a family.

1. Above all, because of the lack of that powerful natural bond which is formed by common parentage, consanguinity, and family love.

2. On account of the greater number of its members.

The greater number renders penetration into the inner life of each individual member more difficult.

3. The pupils are not in the boarding school during their entire youth, but only during a part of it. Strange circles of ideas derived in earlier years may easily produce a contradiction between the views of the family and those of the institution—a contradiction which may prove to be a great obstruction to the process of fusion.

4. Old pupils are constantly departing, and their places being supplied by an influx of new ones.

Despite these obvious differences, education in the boarding school will yet always find the ideal which it must emulate, in the family. It must strive to be able to say with Pestalozzi: "Our children are one with us in heart and soul. They adhere with their whole heart to all our actions. On the whole the spirit of a great domestic union rules, in which, in accordance with the needs of such a union, a pure, paternal and fraternal sentiment shines forth everywhere."

Above all, it should be the aim of these special educational institutions to attain correctness and consistency in their pedagogical arrangements. In such institutions physical education must combine regularity and simplicity with physical freshness and vigour for the purpose of strengthening and hardening the muscles; the instruction must be forcible, adapted to the individual, and capable of awakening interest. The guidance of the pupils must be strong and benevolent, making a wise application of the corporate element.

If the boarding schools and other similar special

educational institutions strive to attain such a high aim, and are thoroughly imbued with a pedagogical spirit, the saying that they are only necessary evils is not tenable; for they may really become nurseries of pedagogical thought and activity, and may thus render great services to science. A glance at the history of pedagogy, in fact, will easily show what great reforms in the sphere of education have emanated from such private institutions. The freedom of organization which these institutions have retained in spite of State supervision, is able in many cases to give impulse to new researches and new experiments—a privilege which is, in fact, more and more denied the establishments of the State. At all events it is wrong to conclude that these institutions are warrantable, merely because, as is alleged, "the family of to-day has lost the love and power for education." This statement fortunately is a strong exaggeration; for if it were true that our families have deteriorated, there would be little to hope for in the future of our people. The motive for the separation of the children from the family during a series of years does not lie merely in the fact that the families have become weaker, but that the relations in which they stand, especially in the larger cities, have become more intense, so that but little strength is left for the education of the children. In this case, in view of the highly developed methods of transacting the affairs of life, and in view of the incapacity of certain families, boarding schools certainly appear to be welcome educational institutions. If, however, they labour only with a view of earning money, if the head of such an establishment merely proposes to accumulate property as rapidly as possible, if these institutions simply stand upon the same footing with commercial interests, then their pedagogical qualifications may be very justly disputed. The farther they remove themselves from the pedagogical ideal, so much the more questionable do they render the work of education in such special institutions.

Classification.

We may distinguish the different institutions that aim to furnish a substitute for home education, according to the various needs that have led to their establishment.

1. The need of giving children a better, more effective education than the paternal home is able to offer under unfavourable circumstances and strained relations, led to the establishment of *boarding schools for the education of boys and girls.*

2. *Consideration of the future career* led to the establishment of *military and clerical schools*, and *normal* or *elementary training schools* for teachers.

3. The *early loss* of *parents* led to the foundation of *orphan asylums*, which as benevolent institutions, justify themselves.

4. *Neglect* of the *primary education* on account of the unfortunate lot of the child required the *reform school*, or the *house of correction*.

5. Those unfortunate children that have some *mental defect* require *asylums* for the *feeble-minded*, and institutions for their *cure* and *instruction*.

6. *Deficiency* or *want* of one of the two higher senses, requires asylums for the *deaf* and *dumb*, and for the *blind*.

INSTITUTES THAT FURNISH A SUBSTITUTE FOR THE FAMILY.

1. Boarding Schools for Boys and Girls.	2. Clerical, Military and Elementary Training or Normal Schools.	3. Orphan Asylums.	4. Reform Schools or Houses of Correction.	5. Asylums for the Feeble-minded.	6. Asylums for the Deaf, Dumb, and Blind.

Institutions for the cure and instruction of the morally, mentally, or physically unsound.

[Some of the above also appear as public institutions, of course.]

3. *Of School Education.*[1]

Society seeks to accomplish the task of its own culture in two directions: (1) by the establishment and maintenance of educative[2] schools and (2) by the establishment of professional schools. The former seek to impart a general culture, the latter to qualify one for some definite calling. The relation between

---

[1] School education here signifies education in the *public* schools as opposed to the schools that have just been described.—*T*'s.

[2] In this translation the use of the words *education, educative,* and *educational*, conforms closely to that of the corresponding German words (*erziehung, erzieherisch, erziehend,* etc.). Accordingly, "education implies not so much the communication of knowledge, as the discipline of the intellect, the establishment of the principles and the regulation of the heart" (Webster).—*T*'s.

the two is defined in the following fundamental proposition: No one should pass from the educative school to the professional school too early, but on the contrary, a comprehensive general education must furnish a foundation for the special professional training, that is as broad as possible and of sufficient depth. If this thorough general education is not furnished, the mental horizon will be prematurely narrowed, and the many-sided interest blunted. As an inevitable consequence, prejudiced and mechanical heads are produced, and the class of society that receives them acquires only clumsy workmen.

To the professional schools belong the agricultural, mining, industrial, and commercial schools, schools of forestry, military and naval schools, normal or elementary training schools for teachers, the polytechnica and the universities.

The educative institutions are erected, so to speak, in three different stages, which consist of the people's schools,[1] the middle schools, and the higher schools. None of these schools aim to prepare for a special *calling* but only to qualify one thoroughly for some definite *sphere* of labour in society. Although, as we shall see, the sphere within which each imparts a general education is narrower in one case or broader in another, all educative schools, both the larger and the smaller, the higher and the lower, still have but one common aim,—to bring the human nature in the pupil to the greatest possible perfection. The desire for knowledge, thought, sympathy, patriotism, and religious interest should be aroused in the scholar of

---

[1] Volksschule.—*T*'s.

the smallest village school just the same as in the scholar of one of the higher schools. Both in the lower and in the higher schools, education has recourse to that circle of thought which arises from intercourse with fellowmen as well as to that which arises from intercourse with Nature. Where education aims to cultivate the whole man, it will always have its ethical and its realistic[1] sides, which are mutually complementary. Every educative school will endeavour to have the contemplation of religious things become a necessity to the scholar, communion with Nature a source of the purest joy, the society of great historical personages an elevation, the devotion to everything beautiful and noble a re-creation, and the search and struggle for clearness and truth a hearty purpose. Such a general education is a pledge that, despite all differences and all separation as regards their calling, fellow-countrymen will still understand, support, and tolerate one another; for they have all gone forth from the educative school, which is the guardian of the most valuable ideal treasures of the family, community, State, and Church. The unity of the educative school, therefore, lies in the common purpose which it always has in view. The differences in its organization arise from the various classes into which society divides, in order to meet the manifold needs of life. These classes which develop within the large social body are usually designated as the lower, middle, and upper, according to the degree of culture which their employment in society demands. From this division into civil classes arises the gradation of

---

[1] As opposed to "humanistic."—*Tr's.*

the educational system. First a clear and definite sepcration of the professional schools from the schools of general culture is to be established; the latter are then to be divided into three forms, graded as follows: The people's school, the real-school, and the higher schools, *i.e.* the higher real-schools and the gymnasia.

The latter aim on the one hand — higher real-schools — to give a suitable preparatory education for the higher institutions of technical instruction, polytechnicum, schools of mining, forestry, etc.; on the other hand (gymnasia), to prepare the child for entrance into a learned profession by introducing him to scientific work. The education which is imparted in the gymnasium is historical, in so far as it goes back to the *sources* of the national culture. In contrast with the gymnasium, the people's school is built entirely upon a national basis, and serves the more extensive strata of society, the working-classes in the more restricted sense,—the peasant, the mechanic, etc. The middle school or real-school embraces in its sphere the modern European culture in order to qualify thorough workmen for commerce, industry, and the lower offices in the Civil Service, and thus to meet the needs of the extensive middle strata of the people. As the "simple real-school," it gives instruction in one foreign language, and retains the scholar up to the sixteenth year, while as the "higher real-school," it gives instruction in two foreign languages and retains the scholar up to the eighteenth year, that he may be able to meet higher requirements. Particulars concerning these forms will be given in subsequent divisions. It is only necessary here to call further attention to the fact that the division of schools here proposed appears as *uncommonly simplified* in comparison with the numerous forms of schools that are now actually prevalent. Have we not now higher and lower burgher-schools, upper real-schools, real-gymnasiums, and real-schools, middle schools, pro-gymnasiums, real-pro-gymnasiums, etc.? Do these different kinds of schools correspond to the actual, distinct needs of civil society? This would, at least, be very difficult to prove. A retrospective glance at the development of these numberless school species, ranging from the people's school to the gymnasium, would show on the contrary how insalutary the excessive number of these creations is, and how necessary it is to remove them, or to transform and reconstruct them into schools that do not owe their existence to incidental purposes, but on the contrary draw their vitality from an inner right of existence.

How blind or how narrow-minded the school administration appears when it is unable to free the school and society from a "false latinity," and permits an unlimited system of privileges,[1] with its evils, to continue. Is it pedagogically and economically justi-

---

[1] The expression, "unlimited system of privileges" refers to the unwholesome practice that has in many cases found its way into the German gymnasia, of granting certain rights in civil and public life to pupils that have advanced to a certain point. The privileges are *graded*, as it were, the greatest privileges requiring the greatest number of years. For example, a youth receives the right to but one year's compulsory military service three years before finishing the gymnasium, and there is no inducement for him to complete his course.—*T*'s.

fiable to send a large number of scholars into life with an imperfect Latin education? What can be the purpose in compelling scholars to study Latin in spite of the fact that they have no need of it whatever, and that Latin is of no value to their culture? The history of the real-school [1] is a history of suffering. That which should have been the real-school, and which should impart a general education for those callings that are not classed among the learned professions, became a pseudo-classical school by the introduction of Latin, and was driven into a contest with the gymnasium that has struck deep wounds into the national life itself, and separated the learned class into two parties.

We can only recover from these unsound conditions by the simplification and readjustment of the separate educational elements in the proper lines. The transformation, as it seems to us to be required, is presented again in the following brief synopsis:—

---

[1] The true real-school represents the progress of realism in education, i.e. it fosters sciences, mathematics, and the modern languages in addition to the common branches of the people's schools. The opposite tendencies are represented by the gymnasium, which is devoted chiefly to the humanities, i.e. to classic learning. The attempts to combine these two lines of culture has given rise to the long series of school species named above, which differ from one another chiefly in the proportion of Latin that is mixed with the course.—*T's.*

ORGANIZATION OF THE EDUCATIONAL SYSTEM.

(A) Educative Schools.

I. Volk's School.
(a) 1-5 School year: General Foundation-School. *Common Sub-structure* for all kinds of schools.
(b) 6-8 School year: People's School, *Super-structure*.

Working-class, in the narrower sense : peasant, mechanic, day-labourer.

II. Middle School.
Real-School, English or French. 6-10 School year.

Retail trade, Industry, lower public or civil offices.

III. Higher Schools.
(a) *Upper Real-School*, French and English. 6-12 School year.

(b) *Gymnasium*, Greek, Latin, French, English. 6-12 School year.

Agricultural, Mining, Industrial, Commercial, Military and Naval Schools, Schools of Forestry, Post Schools, Normal or Elementary Training Schools, Polytechnicum and University.

University (Military and Polytechnicum).

(B) Professional Schools.

Agricultural, Mining, Industrial, Commercial, Military, and Naval Schools ; Schools of Forestry ; Normal or Elementary Training Schools ; Polytechnicum, University. (Only a certificate testifying to the *completion* (*Reife-zeugnis*) of the course given in the educative institutions named under II. and III. should give the right to but one year's military service.)

[Let us make a brief comparison with the schools of the two great English-speaking nations. The German people's or Volk's school corresponds very closely to the English elementary school, or the American common public school. The real-schools and upper real-schools in Germany correspond in general to the English middle-class schools of the second and third grades, and the *modern* first grade schools, or the scientific course in the best American high schools. The German gymnasium corresponds to, but stands somewhat higher than, the *classical* first grade schools of England, including the great public, most grammar and proprietary schools, or the classical course in the best high schools of the United States. The English and German schools are also alike in separating the scholars according to the sphere of life they expect to enter much earlier than do the American schools. In the latter case, for example, the child completes the common school before entering upon classical studies in the high school, preparatory to entering college. In both England and Germany, he begins either classics or modern language much earlier. In Germany, the "common substructure" that all are supposed to receive, now generally occupies three years; the author proposes to lengthen the time to five years. In this respect he and others approach somewhat nearer to the American practice. On the other hand a tendency manifests itself in America at present to apply the English and German practice to some extent, and give the child the opportunity of commencing his philological studies earlier, so as to make his college career more effective. The author also deviates from the actual state of affairs in Germany in rejecting the majority of the school species, and retaining but four, which are based upon the historical development of the German educational system.—*V. L.*]

(*a*) *The People's School.*

The conceptions of "leader" and of "the led," of "the cultured" and "the common people," from which we so often proceed, should not be intensified to artificial antithesis, but should be adjusted so as to produce a natural harmony. It is the highest purpose of all individual and national education not to disunite, but to reconcile, to strengthen well the feeling of national fellowship, and to awaken a consciousness that in a powerful body all members must be thoroughly united. The distinctions of class and calling vanish before this ideal aim. Only men meet men; the high and low, the rich and poor do not contend with one another, but are consciously engaged in a common national work. Therefore when the question of the people's school is under discussion, the conception that a gulf exists between the so-called people's and the higher schools should not be permitted to enter; on the contrary, the people's school should be spoken of as the broad and safe foundation upon which the stately structure of the entire educational system is erected. The whole structure is to be conceived of as a unit, and each part is to be regarded only as an organic member of the whole; unjust pride should be repelled, and to everyone should be awarded the esteem that is due him as a member of the whole. Hence, from the standpoint of the education of the entire people, of the upper, middle, and lower strata, contempt for the people's school gives evidence of very little statesmanlike, sociologic or political insight.

Moreover, this under-valuation is quite unwarranted for the reason that the sphere of the people's school is distinguished by especial advantages. In the midst of the hot contests of the present, the people's school stands as an institution that is recognised on all hands and surely and firmly established. A highly gratifying fact! The people's school should indeed furnish the firm foundation upon which the entire structure of national education is erected; but where the foundation has once been firmly and safely laid, a great deal has already been accomplished. Judicious statesmen and pedagogs, therefore, have, above all, placed the greatest value upon the education of the common people; they have made all national progress and higher culture depend upon the wholesome fundamental education of the entire body. The desire to erect the educational structure from above toward the foundation, bears evidence of very limited insight. Whenever this is the case the endeavour to dazzle the world and to be much talked about prevails over the desire to promote the real welfare of the people. It is true that the often toilsome labour in the people's school is concealed from the view of the multitude; frequently only later decades express their thankfulness to the one who denied himself many a subjective desire and inclination and gave himself thus to the service of the people. The fact that at all times there have been highly gifted men who did not consider it unworthy of their energies to devote their entire strength to the elevation of the people's school, has contributed to that healthy, steady growth of these schools in which Germany rejoices. Though often slighted by their contemporaries, these patriots have still kept on with their retired labours, and succeeding generations have thanked them for it. So many valuable results have been handed down to the present through their exertions, that one can speak quite justly of a permanent possession and of a certain stability and solidity of the entire system.

The period of education in the people's school for both boys and girls includes eight school years, or from the sixth to the fourteenth year of life. It is then followed by a complemental course which extends through two years. The organization of the people's school differs greatly according to the size of the community. Beside the ungraded, one-class,[1] village school stand the graded schools in the cities, comprising from two to eight classes. As regards the course of instruction, since the standpoint has been overcome that sought to keep the people in ignorance under pretence of wholesome restraint, and its representatives have come to wonder at their own brutality, the normal or full number of branches has been reached, including the introduction of drawing and gymnastics, which are obligatory. The introduction of manual training for boys, in both garden and workshop, is a gratifying progress, although it is not yet by any means in that close connection with the other instruction which is to be desired. In general there is a strong effort to place both instruction and school life more thoroughly in the service of education, inasmuch as the training schools for teachers are zealously striving to keep pace with the progress in pedagogics and to train competent educators of the people.

To be sure, a great many things that might be desired still remain in the background. Inasmuch as an education of the people which is based upon the

---

[1] One-class. *i.e.* under one teacher. *T".s.*

principles of the family and adheres to the exclusiveness of personal convictions, must preserve the uniform character of the school even with respect to religion, and, therefore, cannot regard the joint-school [1] as the ideal; it must emphasise its freedom of movement within the limits of the religious confession, and defend itself sharply against all didactic materialism. If, on the one hand, the people's school gladly works hand in hand with the Church as that ideal factor which is its natural ally, it must, on the other hand, vigorously reject all religious guardianship. The independence of the people's school has also already been recognized in several German states, and an exact separation of the sphere of the Church from that of the school has been carried out to the advantage of both.

Furthermore, a transformation of the training schools for teachers is desirable, such as will remove their mixed character, so that the general education will be provided for more thoroughly before the professional education begins.

Particular emphasis is to be placed upon an arrangement of all classes of the educative school according to which, during the first five years, the people's school receives and educates all children from all classes and conditions of life that are of school age. This is what is meant by the demand that the

---

[1] In German "paritätische" or "Simultan-schule," a school which is formed by the joint-agreement of the families of all confessions, wherever the village or town is too small or poor to support a separate school for each confession; the religious instruction is imparted to the children of each confession by the respective pastor.- *Tr*s.

people's school shall lay the foundation for all kinds of schools. After the completion of the five years' elementary course the pupils separate and betake themselves to the different schools, namely, the people's school in its higher work, the higher city school, the real school, or the gymnasium, all of which build further upon this substructure. Such a common foundation as this would result in rich blessings for all. Its benefits would be still further enhanced if each class of scholars could be guided through the different school years by one and the same educator,— a principle whose application in other schools would prove a benefit to education.

Finally, it should also be pointed out that wherever the families are not able to devote the necessary care to their little ones on account of the struggle for daily bread the kindergartens established in the spirit of Pestalozzi and Froebel are to be offered as welcome institutions in which children may be taught to accustom themselves to order, decorum and fitting employment, and where they may begin to cultivate feelings of interest in the prosperity or misfortune of their fellow-beings.

(b) *The Real-Schools.*

As has already been shown, we distinguish two forms of the real-school, a lower and a higher. The former includes six, the latter nine school years.[1] In the former,—the simple "real-school,"—one foreign language is taught, either French or English; in the latter—the higher "real-school"—two foreign languages

---

[1] Which is the present usage, differing from the author's propositions on page 26.

are taught—French *and* English. A certificate showing the course in either one of these institutions to have been completed, should guarantee the right to but one year's military service. While the simple real-school aims to impart an education exclusively for the middle-class of citizens in the cities, the higher real-school should prepare the child for all those callings that are not learned professions (in the more restricted sense), *i.e.* the sciences, forestry, mining, and architecture, the higher postal service, the wholesale commercial life, manufacturing, and the military career; they should also prepare for entrance into the training school for teachers and the polytechnicum. Those who have finished the course of the higher real-school should not be refused the privilege of attending the universities.

The advantages of this organization are manifest. Those callings for which Latin appears to be entirely superfluous and unimportant, are provided with a preparatory school which possesses a distinct character of its own, and which corresponds best to their purposes in each line. By this means the matter of preparatory education ceases to be strained. The gymnasiums are at once freed from all unnecessary ballast, from all those scholars that never intended to devote themselves to a strictly-learned profession. This arrangement would be of twofold, infinite benefit (1) to the scholars who no longer have to torment themselves with useless studies, and (2) to the gymnasiums that no longer have to be troubled with the reluctant pupils, who prematurely and joyfully turn their backs upon the school as soon as some definite privilege has been obtained.

If the education of the people is to be restored again to a healthy condition, the organization of the school must also be directed into judicious, *i.e.* simple, channels. May this view soon prevail and the saying not prove true that, "in Germany two hundred years are necessary to abolish a folly—the first hundred to become aware of it, and the second to remove it."

(c) *The Gymnasium.*

"Die jetzige Menchheit sänke unergründlich tief, wenn nicht die Jugend durch den stillen Tempel der grossen alten Zeiten und Menschen den Durchgang zu dem Jahrmarkt des Lebens nähme."

JEAN PAUL.

Up to the present time the gymnasium has been comparatively stable and unquestioned. Changes in the chief determinative factor, the cultural ideal of the educated circles, take place but very slowly. As soon as they have appeared, however, they also seek to make their influence felt upon the organization of the school system.

It is obvious that at present *two powerful tendencies* are active, both of which are alike unfavourable to the idea of the gymnasium: (1) the rapid progress of the *natural sciences* and the strong realistic trend of the time; (2) the strengthening of the *national feeling* since the re-establishment of the Empire.

In the first case the cultivation of the classic languages is attacked; it is claimed that as dead languages they seem to be useless and signify only a refuted point of view. In the second case learned culture is to be placed only upon a national basis. Both views are equally one-sided and destructive. The old antithesis of humanism and realism has reappeared in all its sharpness. This contest has become so much the more significant because the deficiencies that appear in the curriculum and instruction of the gymnasium have incited even the adherents and representatives of classic culture to sharp criticism. The most important objection which has been brought forward, is that the gymnasium has deteriorated to a preparatory school for classical philologists, whereas it should be the preparatory *educative* institution for all learned professions, and give the pupil the foundation for a deeper grasp of the national life both in its individuality and in its connection with the entire development of the European people. The ideal province of the gymnasium must be constantly and repeatedly emphazised in opposition to the utilitarian tendencies of the present. The representative of such a standpoint should always be met by the words of Aristotle: "Always to consider that which is merely advantageous is unworthy of the free and liberal-minded man."

If we review the attacks that have recently been made upon the gymnasium, and the discussions concerning its reform, we find the following objections:—

1. The physical health is compromised. Certain governmental decrees are directed against the overworking and straining of the eyes, it is true, but without success. Physical exercises are too little cultivated.

2. Much more fatal is the accusation that the

mental health is endangered. It is claimed that the evil lies, in fact, in the wrong method of instruction, which aims at a one-sided philological culture, and culminates in the idea expressed in the well-known saying: "The gymnasium stands or falls with the Latin composition (which has now been removed)." The following points are also criticized in particular:—

(*a*) The grammatical stylistic element preponderates.

(*b*) The miseries of the extempore composition cast their dark shadows over the family.

(*c*) Serious moral injuries make their appearance; impiety and frivolity increase.

(*d*) The results in linguistic instruction are very limited; especially the results of the instruction in German are very impeachable. One observes in the pupils of the gymnasium more frequently than formerly an awkwardness in grammatical expression and deficiency in independent judgment.

(*e*) There is a very apparent deficiency in the philosophical and pedagogical culture of the teachers in the gymnasium. The requirements in this line in the "Examen pro. fac. doc." are also exceedingly limited.

But all these accusations are after all not yet dangerous, for the reason that they do not threaten the existence of the gymnasium. They only criticize, but do not revolutionize. The latest attacks go still further and are directed chiefly against the curriculum. They claim that the exhaustive pursuit of classical antiquity is sheer nonsense; therefore, away with the dead languages. Others desire to limit the study of ancient classics to so great an extent that it would amount to a dissolution of the gymnasium.

We cannot give our consent to such radical measures. The characteristic feature of classical culture consists in adherence to the foundations upon which modern culture has developed. This is necessary for a deeper comprehension of the national life, both in its individuality and in its connection with the entire European culture. As has already been shown, the lower strata of the nation whose task in life can never consist in the furtherance of intellectual culture, receive an education that is based upon the national development. But the education of the middle-classes preserves the connection with the culture of neighbouring peoples. The education of the learned circles follows the historical development of culture from the classical peoples down to the present. The man of learning should circumnavigate the world of culture; we grant him the privilege of an intellectual flight to France and England; but the man of the people we retain at home. No one can fitly promote the intellectual culture of the nation through his own self-activity, who has not acquired a broad historical education. This is what the gymnasium aims to impart; it is a necessary work. Herbart has already called our attention emphatically to the fact that we must retain a firm and vigilant hold of the historical chains of events by means of which we trace back the origin of our culture, so that they shall not escape us. If no other nation were to do this, it should still be the duty of the German nation both for itself and for all others. But the work must be done by all means if we do not wish to bring about a deterioration of the educational condition of the people. Whoever desires this should place himself on the side of the radical utilitarians; but he who wishes to retain the ideal foundations of both our higher culture, and the higher instruction of the youth, must take his stand in favour of the maintenance of the gymnasium. We certainly do not desire to maintain the gymnasium, however, in its present management, which is evidently suffering from certain abuses. If this were not the case, the force of the last shock could not be comprehended. Hence one is obliged to decide either in favour of or against certain reasonable reforms, which should be more thorough-going, however, than the latest Prussian statutes. We should like to see these carried out in the following points:—

1. The re-organisation of the gymnasium should extend first to the training of the teachers. In what lines a change should be made will be shown in the division entitled "Training of Teachers."

2. The elementary preparatory course, which now embraces three years, is not suitable to the purpose; the pupils begin the acquisition of a foreign language before they have made any respectable advance in their mother tongue; hence the necessity of providing a broader foundation which shall comprise the first five years of the people's school.

3. Greek must be placed in the foreground, since, from a pedagogical point of view, the importance of the Roman literature cannot vie in the least with that of Grecian literature.

4. Absorption in the *contents* of the classical work should be the principal task. The grammar should

not be pursued for its own sake, but only in so far as it is necessary to impart an understanding of the writings.

5. The fiction of "formal education"[1] must be given up. In general, there is no such education at all; there exist simply as many kinds of formal education as there are essentially different spheres of intellectual employment.

6. The Latin composition, the extempore productions in their present degenerate form, and the translation from the mother tongue, should all be set aside. The amount of time devoted to instruction in languages may be considerably shortened (making due allowance for the aim stated in No. 4), in order to make room for other educational elements.

7. The esthetic element, which is of such fundamental importance in grasping the antique world, must be brought to the front in some effective manner. It is fostered by the introduction of instruction in art and drawing from the lowest to the highest grades.

8. Physical training must be undertaken in a far more effectual manner than is at present the case.

9. Much more time must be granted the realistic

---

[1] "Formal education" or "formal culture," signifies about the same as the vague expression, "discipline of the mind." Its extreme defendants claim that the pursuit of classic studies renders the intellect capable in any sphere whatever, *i.e.* it develops *all* the mental faculties. It is true that the study of a language renders the pursuit of other related branches easier; but it cannot be conceded that it prepares the mind directly for grasping other totally irrelevant subjects.—*T's.*

branches (natural sciences, mathematics, geography), and their pursuit must be much more energetic.

10. The final or departing examination (*Abiturientenexamen*) should be set aside. The privilege of conferring a certificate, testifying to the completion of the course, and necessary for admittance to the polytechnicum, university, etc., should be granted the board of teachers.

11. Freedom should also be granted the board of teachers in the formation of the curriculum as to its individual features, in so far as this does not conflict with certain general standards.

12. The recently introduced "intermediate examination" (*Zwischenexamen*[1]) should be energetically opposed, in order that it may be removed as soon as possible. It sunders the curriculum of *one* school into *two* irreconcilable parts.

There is not space here to give sufficient grounds for the establishment of these claims. They are presented, in part at least, by others, and approach most closely to the views that have found expression in the German Einheits-schulverein.[2] (Hannover.) The following outline may serve to give a summary of the chief tendencies in this line of school reform :—

---

[1] This intermediate examination refers to the system o privileges already mentioned on page 27 and in the accompanying footnote. It occurs at the completion of "unter secunda," three years before the close of the regular gymnasium course.— T"s.

[2] An association for a union-school. See L. R. Klemm, *The Movement for an Einheits-schule in Germany*, in the *Educational Review*, vol. i, No. 4, N. Y.--T"s.

GYMNASIUM.

(A) Conservative Standpoint.	(B) Mediatorial Standpoints.			(C) Radical Standpoint.
	1. Moderate Reform.	2. More Progressive Reform.		Extreme Utilitarians.
		Bifurcation Systems.		
Desires to retain the Gymnasium in its present condition. Representatives: Wendt, Jäger und Uhlig. Periodical: Uhlig, "das humanistische Gymnasium." (The Humanistic Gymnasium.) Heidelberg, 1890.	"Der Deutsche Einheitsschulverein." (The German Association for a Union School.) Horniemann, Periodicals of the same association, Nos. 1-7, Hannover.	1. Association: "Neue deutsche Schule." (New German School.) Berlin. Periodical: Göhring, "N. dtsch. Schule." (New German School.) Hamburg. 1st Stage. 6-14 yr. English in 10th yr. 2nd Stage. 14-16 yr. French in 12th yr. 3rd Stage. 16-20 yr. Greek 4 years and Latin 3 years. For philologists and theologians.	2. "Association for School Reform," Berlin. Lange, Periodical "f. d. Reform d. höh Schl." (For the Reform of the Higher Schools.) Braunschweig. Middle School of 6 years. Latin and Greek faculties. Then 3 schools with 3 years each. 1. Gymnasium. 2. Real-Gymnasium. 3. Upper Real-School.	No Classic Languages whatever. Only the Modern Languages and the Natural Sciences.

(d) *The System of Girls' Schools.*

While the school system for boys has exhibited a remarkable abundance of organizations, we also find certain diversities among the educational institutions for girls, it is true, but they may all be reduced essentially to three kinds of schools. The first runs parallel with the people's school for boys, and closes with confirmation; the second goes far beyond this goal, and corresponds to the higher city-school[1] for boys; it gives instruction in one foreign language, generally French. This is an excellent arrangement for educating the daughters of the cultured citizens, of officials of the middle-class and of merchants, although it is not yet sufficiently carried out. The third kind, the higher school for girls, aims to impart a higher culture by lengthening the period of attendance at school to the sixteenth year, by deepening the instruction, and cultivating two foreign languages. It is sometimes succeeded also by the seminary for the training of lady teachers, as the highest grade, in order that those young girls who desire may prepare themselves for teaching.

The views concerning the organization, nature, and aim of the higher schools for girls are comparatively harmonious, although a certain tendency has recently become noticeable in womens' associations to regard the higher schools for girls more as institutions on a level with the gymnasium. The aim, therefore, is to further the development of intelligence and the amassment of a great deal of knowledge. This tendency

---

[1] *Bürgerschule.—T's.*

purposes to carry learning into the feminine world in order to render women capable of participating in as many different professions and callings as possible, even in those which have heretofore been exclusively in the hands of the men. New spheres of activity are to be opened to the energy of women; the struggle for existence is to be lightened. In opposition to this tendency, another view adheres to the conviction that the girl should be educated not for the world and its affairs, but for the home and its management, even if she is not refused entrance to certain professions, such as that of the educator and the physician. However, intellectual culture should not always stand in the foreground, but rather an ethical culture, and the culture of the heart. The cultured classes in Germany do not need women of great learning, reading, and versatility so much as, in preference to all else, mothers, who possess a clear insight into the world and are capable of following the affairs of the husband with the keenest interest; who are stout-hearted and can animate the entire family life with that warmth which is necessary for a cheerful prosperity; who devote their energies to the household, rule affectionately and zealously in this limited sphere, and are at the same time sufficiently strong and healthy to undertake the task. The first mentioned tendency, which happily has few adherents among male and female teachers, is more theoretical; the latter is thoroughly practical. The cultivation of the intellect is the chief aim of the former; the cultivation of the heart the highest aim of the latter, which does not seek knowledge for its own sake, but only in so far as it enters into the service of a strong personal character. Without doubt the second view is far more in accord with the German sentiment than the first, which derives its nourishment chiefly from theories that are introduced from abroad. Otherwise it will probably only be a question of time until the German university is also freely opened to very gifted young ladies for scientific studies, especially medicine and pedagogy.

As regards the length of the curriculum in the higher schools for girls, the so-called Berlin normal plan fixes upon nine years in opposition to the far greater number of ten-year-schools. The latter possess an advantage that is not to be undervalued, in that they retain the same scope of work, and hence do not need to increase the amount of instruction for each year as the nine-year-schools are compelled to do.

In 1872, certain well-known representatives of the higher schools for girls assembled in Weimar, founded an association in the interest of these schools,[1] and in a memorial document laid the demands of the association before the several governments of the German States. For two years this association has found an ally in the "Prussian association," which has undertaken the special task of substituting a better course of study for the Berlin plan of 1886, and of working for the legal regulation of the system of girls' schools in Prussia. The German association pursues chiefly the more general ideal aims; the Prussian association chiefly the practical aims.

[The above section has brought out a characteristic feature of the German school. With the exception of the one-class

---

[1] Verein für höhere Mädchenschulen.—*T's.*

village schools, the co-education of the sexes is almost wholly unknown. The same is true in general of English schools (exclusive of Scotland); whereas, in America, co-education, or mixed education, is the rule. The salutary effects of mixed education cannot be doubted; the few instances, where it has been tried in Germany and other countries, have given the greatest satisfaction.—*V. L.*]

(B) OF SCHOOL ADMINISTRATION.

The school administration has, in general, four tasks to fulfil, viz. the foundation, maintenance equipment, and supervision of the school system, including the preparation of teachers for the various kinds of schools. Accordingly we shall discuss—

1. *School Legislation.*

The question of school legislation has lapsed into ineffable confusion owing to the deficient grasp of the situation in its objective phases, and to complication with the party conflicts of politics and the Church. Some reject every proposal for a reformation, at least if it does not aim at assisting in a still more rigorous application of their principles. But just that view has thus far been unable to obtain a hearing in public transactions, which has been quietly and scientifically developed in smaller circles. In fact, a pronounced partiality appears even among teachers themselves, in so far as they are sturdily endeavouring to place themselves under the authority of the State. They look to the State for the fulfilment of all their desires, for the elevation of their social position, and a liberal income. Furthermore, certain political parties give them distinctly to understand that, as soon as they have attained political power, all demands made by the teaching profession shall be granted. The settlement of the question, which, in fact, must be regarded as a difficult one, is only still further disconcerted by such egotistical endeavours.

We have to consider here a matter of no less importance than the adjustment and impartial combination of the claims of different factors, all of which have a natural interest in the educational system. It is not unraveling the knot, but simply severing it, when the almighty power of the State is raised to the throne without further ceremony, and the privilege of taking a self-active part in the development of the school system is denied all other factors. This cannot happen without damage to the interests of the schools themselves, which, like all other intellectual movements, thrive so much the better the greater the number of active factors that participate in their advancement. Without doubt, the family possesses the most natural right; next to the family stand the community and the Church. It is the task of school legislation to establish the right relation between the State and these three factors. It should guarantee to each individual sphere both the opportunity and a sufficiently free scope for the appearance of its natural interests, which, as such, are very deeply rooted. All legislation which does not take natural interests into consideration will sow the seeds of constant strife, and never preserve the ardour that characterizes a growing organism bearing healthy fruit.

As we have already repeatedly shown, the family is the natural bearer of the first and highest interests of education therefore, education must proceed from the family. The fundamental presupposition of all school legislation consists in the recognition of the rights of the family in education. This right must be considered before that of all other participants, and the proportionate influence of the separate factors will be determined accordingly. The organization begins with the establishment of local school communities, or districts, which are alliances of families whose members acknowledge one and the same educational ideal. In conjunction with the civic, State, and ecclesiastical organizations of society, they are then to be combined into the broader school communities of the "Kreis" and "Provinz," and the School Boards organized accordingly. In all cases those points at which the clearly defined influence of the State or Church is entitled to appear, are to be exactly designated. Such legislation secures the necessary independence of the educational system, which is thus placed on a level with the army, the Church, the judicial department, etc.; it assures a suitable co-operation of all corporate interests, and preserves the national character and the sympathy with the national spirit far more than is possible in a school system that is ruled only by its supreme authorities. Finally, this form of legislation furnishes an effective protection against the vicissitudes of political and social partisanship. It should be further emphasized that, in the formation of the administrative system of the schools, a representative assembly or board should be created in every instance, beside the executive office, *e.g.* the "Schulvorstand" beside the "Schulamt," the "Kreisschulsynode" beside the "Kreisschulinspector," the "Provinzialschulsynode" beside the "Provinzialbehörde," the "Landesschulsynode" beside the "Ministerium."[1]

Such school legislation secures the rights of all interested parties, and guarantees a healthy and vigorously pulsating educational life. In place of the absolute power of the State, therefore, an authority should be recognized, which, although it is not entirely different from the former, and has issued only from the families, nevertheless depends upon their co-operation. Just as the Church thrives best when its families are not made silent co-workers, but are allowed to take an active part in the development of the religious life, so the school can only truly thrive in behalf of the interests of both the family and the State, when the principle of unlimited *State* supervision, or State omnipotence, has been given up.

The following statements set forth our views upon the formation of the school system in accordance with the fundamental principles presented above.

---

[1] In general, the "Kreis," "Provinz," and "Land" correspond respectively to the township, county, and State. To these three is sometimes added a fourth, the "Bezirk" (see page 54), which then corresponds to the township, and the "Kreis" to a city-circuit. According to the above proposition, the school system would comprise four distinct circuits, grading from the school district to the State department of culture, each with its representative and executive departments, as follows:—

(A) *Circuit.*	(B) *Representative Body.*	(C) *Executive Office.*
1. School District.	Schulvorstand.	Schulamt.
2. Kreis.	Kreisschulsynode.	Kreisschulinspector.
3. Provinz.	Provinzialschulsynode.	Provinzialbehörde.
4. Land.	Landesschulsynode.	Ministerium.

The reader can make the necessary comparisons with the school legislation of his State for himself.—*T's.*

I. The School Community.

1. The family possesses the primary and most natural rights, as well as obligations, in respect to the education of the youth.

2. The school can only be regarded as an arrangement made by the families for the common education of their youth. An association of families possessing a common school constitutes a school community.

3. The children, as members of the family who are under age, belong to an ethical-religious, a civil and a political community only *through* their connection with the family. The claims of the Church, of the civil community and of the State upon the child, therefore, can only be indirect, however great and important they may be in themselves.

4. Common education implies that the families concerned, and their professional educators, agree in the most important fundamental educational principles, that they are therefore concordant in matters of conscience.

5. The concordance in matters of conscience, or the common view of life, characteristic of the various members of the school community, has found expression, both historically and legally, in the religious communities recognised by the State—an expression that is confessional, although very much in want of various reforms. It is natural that the school communities, as far as their inner nature is concerned, should be founded upon these religious communities. The schools that stand upon this ground are regarded as public.

6. If families of different confessions, or dissidents,

agree to establish a common school, the State should not refuse to recognise this so-called simultaneous or joint-school as a public institution.

7. Under certain limitations to be determined by the State, single individuals, families, and communities of families must be permitted to establish private schools, provided they are able to give sufficient account of their educational principles.

8. All of the free school communities of a State constitute a common State school system, whose different members, from the lowest to the highest, may be presented as follows:—

    (*a*) Local school community (school district).
    (*b*) School community of the Kreis (Stadt).
    (*c*) School community of the Bezirk.
    (*d*) School community of the Province.

9. All publicly recognized school communities should receive corporate rights, especially the right of self-government. The legislation accordingly should receive a synodical character, in that each single school community has its corresponding board of directors, the Kreis and Bezirk each its special representative body, the province its provincial synod, and the State school system a State school synod.

10. In order that the right of self-government may not remain merely nominal, but become a reality from the local board of school directors up to the State school synod, the various bodies representing the families should be invested with the necessary authority, according to their rank; this arrangement recognizes the truth that a corporate representative body can only develop life when it has some-

thing to determine. The school system can only truly thrive under such a decentralization, for it is then sustained by the work of the entire people. But the State, which retains the chief right of supervision, will only be the gainer by this regulation; the same is true of the Church whose influence in the representative bodies of the school can obtain recognition without being burdened with the odium of making direct encroachments upon the educational system. State, Church, and school should constitute a united force in which the various circles of activity retain their independence, and are mutually effective and sustaining.

II. The Church.

1. The religious communities are to recognize the complete independence of the school communities that have sprung up upon their foundations. Hence they must relinquish all special rights over the school, particularly the right of supervision.

2. The clergyman should be permitted to be present in the school at the religious instruction. If he desires to censure the same in certain particulars, he must report to his superior board, which is to lay the complaints in question before the school synod for decision. The clergyman should not be allowed to interfere directly in the curriculum and the method of religious instruction in the school.

3. Opportunity should be given the clergy in the school synod to make known their pedagogical convictions as regards the curriculum, text-books, and methods of instruction.

4. The Church should be granted the privilege of sending a representative to the State examination of teachers, who is to be allowed a seat and voice in the examining board.

III. THE CIVIL COMMUNITY AND THE STATE.

1. In its external organization the school should be founded upon the civil community, just as its inner life should rest, so far as possible, upon religious communities.

2. The civil community and the State assume the management of the external affairs of the school (construction of school buildings, appointments, salaries, etc.).

3. The State is not authorized, however, to entrench upon the foundations and the nature of the family. Hence it should not think of rendering the school a purely State institution, *i.e.* it should not aim to assume exclusive control of the youth for the benefit of its own designs.

4. The State should have the chief right of school supervision, however. It has the right to demand that education and instruction shall not be neglected, that the schools shall pursue no course hostile to its interests, and that they shall attain certain results which are essential to its task. As regards the latter it should fix upon certain minimum aims to be attained by the various kinds of schools.

5. The State provides for certain educational offices of supervision, which correspond to, assist, and support the School Boards. They are as follows:—

(a) The "Kreis" or "Bezirksschulamt" beside the "Kreis" or "Bezirk" board.
(b) The "Provinzial-Schulrat" beside the "schul-synod" of the province.
(c) The "Oberschulrat" (division for schools in the educational department) beside the "State-school-synod."

6. The State convenes the school synods, superintends the interaction of all factors participating in the school system, and thus provides for the uniform management of the entire educational structure.

7. The State, in common with the representative bodies of the various communities, governs the financial affairs and superintends the proper equalization of the taxes that are levied for the purpose of raising means.

8. The State has the right to close private schools whenever they work in opposition to the national interests and pursue tendencies that are dangerous to the common welfare.

2. *The Equipment of Schools.*

It is the task of the school administration above all to investigate the wants of the school, and to satisfy the same by means of suitable regulations. The chief lines of this duty lie in the provision of *schoolrooms, school apparatus* and *teachers*.

1. School hygiene gives the necessary directions as to the arrangement and structure of schoolrooms. Happily, the efforts of the school administration have been retrieved from a misplaced economy; in fact, the

school buildings in many villages and cities are a splendid ornament. Great progress is noticeable in this direction as compared with former times; the school administrations vie with one another in their endeavours to possess the best arranged school buildings.

2. We also find considerable progress in the line of school apparatus as compared with former times. The most necessary materials for the work of instruction are probably everywhere supplied. Dealers in school apparatus promptly furnish the supplies; school museums afford an excellent survey of the abundant materials for use in all departments of instruction, that are now at the command of the teacher.

3. It is obvious that the greatest care of the school administration is to obtain competent teachers, and to retain them after they have once been employed. Here the stipend undoubtedly has a great influence. The requirement which F. A. Wolf placed upon the teacher, to be always healthy and to know how to endure the severest pangs of hunger whenever and wherever it is necessary, is, forsooth, a very ideal requirement; but it is difficult to see just why teachers, whose very devotion to the education of the youth already requires so much self-denial and the exertion of all the energies, should have to make such a sacrifice. On the contrary, the energy of the educator should be supported as effectually as possible by a liberal stipend. A meagre salary exerts a twofold harmful influence upon the teacher—(1) in so far as it is the cause of troublesome restrictions, want, and care, and (2) in that it drives him to supplementary work in leisure hours. The one is just as harmful as

the other, for both undermine that fundamental frame of mind (joy in the profession and mental serenity) without which the business of the educator cannot thrive. But how shall the teacher's enthusiasm for his work be retained and nourished, even when he has been inspired by the lofty significance of education, if neglect, want, and care are constantly associated with it? The educator should by all means carry on his work only because he has a sincere love for it, never from a base self-interest; there is no labour which stimulates one to bear all kinds of exertion and sacrifice by virtue of its inner worth and lofty significance more than that of the educator. But one cannot live alone upon the greatest inspiration and the most exalted intellectual feasts; even the nature of the most liberal educator must always remain human. It seems, therefore, to be an urgent duty to adjust the social position of the teacher so that it will be proportionate to the importance which society ascribes to the profession of the educator, and to grant him a livelihood so ample that all possibility of dissatisfaction with the external circumstances of life is excluded from the beginning.

3. *Of the Supervision of Schools.*

A system of forces always requires a regulating power, which, in this case, must be found in the sovereignty of the State. It is the duty of the State to guide and superintend the entire school system. This management has, above all, to guard against severity, tyranny, bureaucracy, and the tendency to check spontaneity by the dictation of ready-made formulas, all of which compromise the prosperity of the schools. The French ideal, according to which the Minister of Instruction could boast of being able, watch in hand, to state, on any day whatever, exactly whether the teachers of all the schools in all departments were engaged at a given moment in repetition or dictation, in reading or grammar, does not accord with the German nature. Here personality and individuality must have the free play upon which their efficacy essentially depends. The management should not be felt everywhere as an oppressive burden, but as a friendly service that furthers personal efficiency. Its frequent failure in this respect, however, is due partly to the establishment of final examinations under the supervision of the State, partly to the fact that very unsuitable persons have been chosen for the inspection of the schools. The development of the school system brought about a custom, in accordance with which the State availed itself of ecclesiastical authorities for the inspection of the lower and middle schools. This arrangement was acceptable as long as the school system was still in the beginning of its development. In its present condition, however, the demand is imperative that the inspection of the schools be entirely in the hands of the profession itself, *i.e.* that only those men shall be selected for the management and inspection of the schools that have enjoyed a competent pedagogical training both theoretically and practically.

It should also be emphasized that, with the appointment of professional men to the inspection of schools in the Kreis, and with the formation of smaller districts, the so-called local school inspection may well be dropped.

4. *Of the Training of Teachers.*

In this sphere the school administration has been guilty of remarkable inconsistency. More than a hundred years ago it began to provide for the pedagogical training of teachers for the people's schools, and in the last decades a great deal has been done in this same line. In the meantime the universities have provided more and more liberally for the scholarship of teachers for the middle and higher schools, while their preparation for the future educational task itself has been totally neglected. Learning appeared to be the chief thing; pedagogical and philosophical training was regarded as something unessential. On the contrary, the learning, *i.e.* the general culture of teachers for the people's schools, was neglected, while the pedagogical phase of their training was much more emphasized.

This last statement already indicates in what lines the reformation of the training schools [1] for teachers of the people's schools must be effected. The mixed character, which these institutions now bear, must be removed in favour of professional culture; the teachers' seminary must be advanced to the position of the professional schools. This presupposes, at least, that the preparatory education, which is at present quite insufficient, be considerably broadened and deepened, or that the general education be acquired by finishing the course of an upper real-school. The latter is to be preferred. With the present condition of the teachers' seminaries, neither the general culture nor

---

[1] Volksschullehrerseminar.—*T's.*

the professional pedagogical training receive the proper attention; for this reason the curse of an indifferent culture generally clings to the position of teacher in the people's school. A prudent school administration should leave no stone unturned to remove this reproach.

An important and progressive step has been taken in Prussia as regards the pedagogical training of candidates for positions in the higher schools; a year in the seminary has been introduced before the so-called trial year, and seminaries have been established in connection with a large number of gymnasiums and real-gymnasiums. Previously the pedagogical training of teachers in the higher schools of Prussia had been attempted in two ways: (1) in eleven practical pedagogical seminaries that are separate from the university; (2) in the so-called trial year. The purpose of the latter was to give the great mass of candidates, who could not be admitted into the pedagogical seminaries, at least one year's opportunity for practical preparatory work in teaching. This arrangement was early recognized as wholly insufficient. Even as early as 1849 the general school conference,[1] under the direction of the Minister von Ladenburg, pronounced the trial year to be an inefficient arrangement, but only in 1889 was a step taken to supply the deficiency by the foundation of seminaries in connection with the gymnasiums.

By the side of these, pedagogical seminaries should be organized in the universities for the purpose of training both the teachers that will labour neither in

---

[1] Landesschulconferenz.—*T's.*

the people's schools nor in the gymnasiums (*i.e.* teachers for real-schools, teachers' seminaries, higher girls schools, etc.), and the theologians and school inspectors. But there are other important reasons for the establishment of pedagogical seminaries in the universities.

In general the separation of so important a sphere as the science of education from the living forces of the university, where all the other chief phases of the national culture are carefully nurtured, can certainly be only a detriment to the national development. There is hardly a sphere of labour whose thrift is more easily endangered by mere mechanical conformity to existing practices than that of the schools, if one places any value whatever upon the fresh, energetic, and independent spirit that should pervade them. A judicious school administration will have no dread of such a spirit, but will rather value it highly, because the thrift and success of the education of the youth depends upon the strength of this living spirit. Wherever it has become extinct we shall watch in vain for that fresh, strong, active race that rejoices in and is desirous of work, and of which we stand in so much need. Who would doubt, however, that the cultivation of such an active spirit will thrive best where the freedom of science flourishes? Who would not regard the organization of pedagogical institutes in the universities just as desirable as the establishment of seminaries for teachers in connection with the gymnasiums? The former, under the protection of the freedom of science, should become central points for the cultivation of scientific pedagogics. From them the gymnasium seminaries—which, as members of the State school system, can never enjoy the same freedom of movement, will receive their most effective stimulation and reinvigoration. Hence, if fresh life is to be developed in the teachers' seminaries for both the gymnasiums and the people's schools, the source of nourishment in the universities must not be obstructed, but properly opened.

[The above section upon school administration, although applied directly to German needs, still touches upon problems of universal interest. Most prominent among these is that of the relative power of the family, State, and Church in determining the character of the educational system. In Germany the Church has always possessed great power in educational matters, for the growth of the present school system dates from the first efforts of Luther in behalf of elementary instruction. Its power has waned but little, for the schools are largely confessional, and religious instruction is imparted in all educative schools. The condition was similar in England up to 1870; many of the schools either are still in the hands of Church communities, or were originally founded by the Church. Instruction in religion is the rule. In America the Church has no direct influence upon the public schools; religious instruction is not imparted in them. In all of these countries the rights of the Church and State in education are prominent educational topics.—*V. L.*]

PART II.

Theoretical Pedagogics.

As we have already seen, practical pedagogics cannot dispense with the aid of two fundamental sciences, social ethics and social psychology. Theoretical pedagogics is likewise directed to these same two sciences, but in the form of individual ethics and individual psychology.

The first task which presents itself is to show how the aim of education is to be derived from ethics. This is the task of teleology. As soon as the ends which education has to fulfil, are known, the next question is that of the means by which these aims are to be reached. This question must be decided by that science which treats of the laws to which the inner life of man conforms, *viz.* psychology. It is, therefore, the task of methodology to show how the choice, arrangement and preparation of the intellectual food may be adapted to the psychical laws.

Accordingly, we have the following outline :—

THEORETICAL PEDAGOGICS.

| (A) Theory of the purpose of education. Teleology. (*Ethics.*) | (B) Theory of the means of education. Methodology. (*Psychology*) |

(a) Teleology.

When the educator reflects as to what he shall make of his pupil with reference to human society, the first thought that suggests itself is to investigate the conception of education for the purpose of gaining some hints as to its aim.

Unfortunately, one does not advance very far by this means. The investigation of the conception of education, however, reveals certain real features that are present in the reflections of everyone. But that very little progress can be made by beginning in this manner becomes apparent at once when we briefly review these features :—

1. In the first place, we find that education takes place only with mankind, a fact which Rosenkranz sums up in the following words :—" Man is educated by man for humanity."

2. We know that education does not extend to adults, but is confined to the children. The latter are cared for by their elders. Wherever children are left to themselves, no education takes place.

3. By investigating the conception of education, we learn that the educative activity must be systematic and well arranged, if it is to succeed. Hence Waitz said, " Education is the systematic exertion of an influence upon the inner life of another while it is yet educable."

4. The psychical condition of the pupil should not be influenced merely during the activity of the educator, but should attain a permanent form ; neither should it be affected in spite of, or in conflict with,

his influence. The training which the one that is being educated receives through education should acquire a certain stability and durability.

These thoughts are all very good, but we have not been brought one step nearer the solution of our question, for no hint whatever is contained in the conception of education itself as to what form the character of the pupil should attain, or what training he should receive.

Since the conception of education itself is not able to give definite but only general suggestions, the next thought is to turn to history in order to learn what the true purpose of education is. In so doing, however, one may easily fall into Scylla while trying to avoid Charybdis. Shall the educator follow Rousseau and educate a man of nature in the midst of civilized men? In so doing, as Herbart has shown, we should simply repeat from the beginning the entire series of evils that have already been surmounted. Moreover, it would give the educator as much trouble to make a living in such a heterogeneous society as in after life the one whom he had educated. Or shall we turn to Locke and prepare the pupil for the world, which is customarily in league with worldlings? We should then arrive at the standpoint of Basedow, and aim to educate the pupil so that he would become a truly useful member of human society. Of course we should always be harassed with the secret doubt as to whether this is the ideal purpose after all, and whether we are not at times directly enjoined to place the pupil at variance with the usage and customary dealings of the world. If we reflect that an endless career is open to man for his improvement, we realize that only that education whose aims are always the highest, can hope to reach the lofty goals that mark this career.

Therefore, an ideal aim must be present in the mind of the educator. Possibly he can obtain information and help from Pestalozzi, whose nature evinced such ideal tendencies. Pestalozzi wished the welfare of mankind to be sought in harmonious cultivation of *all* powers. If one only knew what is to be understood by a multiplicity of mental powers, and what is meant by the *harmony* of various powers. These phrases sound very attractive, but give little satisfaction. The purely *formal* aims of education will appeal just as little to the educator: " Educate the pupil to independence ; " or, " educate the pupil to be his own educator ; " or, " educate the child so that it will become better than its educator" (Hermann and Dorothea, Hector and Astyanax in the *Iliad*). Such and similar attempts to fix the purpose of education are abundant in the history of pedagogy; but they do not bring us nearer the goal. In their formal character they do not say, for example, of what kind the independence shall be, what content it shall have, what aims it shall have in view, or in what directions its course shall lie. For the pupil that has become independent can use his freedom rightly for good just as well as misuse it for evil.

If the purpose of education is to possess any real worth, it must, above all else, be of a *concrete* nature; it must indicate the content of the mental training. We have just become acquainted with several formulations which fulfil this condition, as, for example, the eudemonistic principle of Locke and the philanthropists, Rousseau's principle of conformity to nature, and the humanistic principle of Pestalozzi, Herder, Lessing, and others, which culminates in the demand for a "true humanity." To these we can readily add the rationalistic principle, which aims at rationality, enlightenment, and intellectual culture; the orthodox Christian principle, which demands that man, who was created in the image of God but lost through sin, be redeemed (Palmer), and the pietistic principle of Spener, Francke, and Zinzendorf, which aspires to piety and godliness.

Without doubt there is an abundance of examples from which the educator can choose to his heart's content. But, as is well known, he who has the choice also has the vexation that accompanies it.[1] The desire to attain a firm standpoint very soon makes itself felt. How shall he succeed in finding the lofty standpoint upon which he can base his decision with complete inner harmony and contentment, when history submits several aims of education, all of which seem to him to be equally valuable and expedient? Perhaps he can overcome the difficulty by combining these various aims, thus arriving at a plurality of educational purposes which, taken together, are to determine the activity of the educator. Does not the attempt to do justice to all the different standpoints appear to be a happy solution of the difficulty? Is it not advisable, in accordance with the well-known receipt: "Test everything and retain the best," to select and arrange a series of aims from that which is correct in the different tendencies?

---

[1] The German proverb is, "Wer die Wahl hat, hat auch die Qual."—*Ts.*

Thus, for example, let the religious aim be selected from the theological sphere, the taste for nature and simplicity from Rousseau; from Locke and Basedow the regard for one's skill and ability as a useful member of, and active participant in, human society; from Pestalozzi and the humanists the expansion of one's view of life, so that at some future time the pupil can say with Terence: "Nihil humani a me alienum puto."

All this might be very good, were it not for the fact that such a series of aims resemble a mere collection or mass of unordered subordinate thoughts that happen to be pertinent, rather than a well-organized system of properly derived conceptions that are held together by some internal bond, and that may be subsumed under one supreme purpose.

Accordingly, we are justified in maintaining that we should not be content with a multiplicity of educational aims, which undoubtedly correspond to different phases of human activity, but should pass on to a paramount point of view which commands the entire sphere.

Unity of the plan is inconceivable without unity of the aim. We can only hope to master the situation when the plan of education appears as a system of forces which, for years, always pursue one and the same end. If the work of the pedagog is ever to be regarded as, in all respects, a single compact whole, it must also be possible to conceive of the task of education as a unit. Although it is self-evident that the complexity of the work of education requires a multiplicity of aims, it is at the same time just as necessary that the multiplicity of aims, offered by experience, be subsumed under one chief, supreme, educational purpose. The sovereign power of such an aim secures the unity of the pedagogical activity. The need of uniformity is satisfied, the educator is free to devote his energies uninterruptedly to a concentrated activity, in spite of the promptings of a crude empiricism and erroneous theories. All single educational activities must find their support and centre in a single thought which governs them all; no isolated means of education, as such, can be regarded as of any value, except as it receives its worth and significance through certain definite relations which it bears to all other means and to the paramount educational aim. Education can make no use of chief and subordinate purposes which have to make mutual concessions, but only of a single supreme purpose which may be subdivided into a system of subordinate purposes; the latter, on their part, must be so inter-related as to constitute the necessary steps in the attainment of the former.

We recollect that this uniform purpose is to be found with the aid of *ethical* investigations. It appears therefore, that, in order to obtain exact information as to the educational purpose which we desire to establish, we must now turn to ethics.

But a new difficulty arises at once. To *what ethics* should philosophical pedagogy turn? In which form of ethics should it seek its foundation? Should it agree with Schleiermacher in giving up the attempt to attach itself to a definite system of ethics, because there is no system that is recognized by all, and do well to content itself with a general, unsatisfactory answer? This is not our standpoint. Although it is to be granted that no ethical system is yet recognized by everybody, there cannot be any doubt for a moment, however, that but one group of ethical systems should be considered by the educator; this is the group of ethical systems which exclude from the beginning eudemonism in any form. Eudemonism, in whatever form it appears, harbours great dangers. Hence, the conclusion is unavoidable that every ethical system which represents eudemonism, either covertly or openly, is useless for education. Furthermore, a positive utilitarianism which condemns everything with the utmost contempt that is not directly applicable and useful, is always allied with eudemonism. Utilitarianism, however, only creates the new danger that all ideal pursuits will be gradually crowded into the background. This would be followed by the appearance of a general moral torpidity which would render both society and the individual incapable of all higher inspiration, cut off every possibility of cultivating pure ethical characters, and entirely dim the vision for the appreciation of the ideally beautiful and good.

Hence, if the educator desires to place only an ideal aim in view as the goal toward which to aspire, he should not hesitate; he can only have recourse to a system of ethics which does not seek the value of moral endeavour in the object to which it is directed, but in the moral inclinations, in the activity of the will itself. This ideal standpoint seems to have found a clear expression in the ethical system of Herbart which, as the doctrine of the ethical ideas, has been developed upon the foundation obtained through Kant.

This ethics excludes entirely all relative estimation

of worth, *i.e.* all estimation which values the will for the sake of some desired effect, for the sake of some gain. Even the opposers of the Herbartian ethics willingly recognize its grandeur. A system of ethics, they say, which is undertaken with pure devotion to the nature of its problems, which regards the morally beautiful as the highest, sublimest, and noblest end, —an ethics which, like that of Plato, cannot conceive how anyone can behold the morally beautiful without being deeply moved and inspired, which regards it as a matter of course, that that which is morally beautiful will receive the absolute approval of all,—such an ethics will always attract and hold truly ethical minds, despite all differences of presentation and all deviations in fundamental views. On account of its ideal character it will always exercise its power of attraction especially upon educators who desire to pursue an ideal educational purpose. It will not fail to be of assistance to anyone who desires to sketch an ethical ideal that can serve the educator as a supreme educational purpose,—an ideal whose realization in the pupil must be his chief task.

Neither knowledge, nor goods, nor external actions are good in themselves, but only a good will. It must be the person's own will, developed by insight into the absolutely binding validity of the moral law or the absolute beauty of the moral ideal. The Herbartian ethics sketches five of these ethical ideas: the idea of inner freedom, the idea of completeness (efficiency of the will), the idea of goodwill, the idea of rights, and the idea of equity. The idea of *inner freedom* signifies the harmony of the activity of the will with the practical insight, or conscience. The individual will must correspond exactly to the latter, and execute whatever it presents. The idea of *completeness* or of the efficiency of the will demands the many-sidedness, energy, concentration, and the progress of the will. The idea of *goodwill* manifests itself in unselfish devotion to the welfare and a practical sympathy for the woe of others. The idea of *rights* culminates in the demand to avoid strife (mutual recognition of rights). Finally, the idea of *equity* looks to the impartial adjustment of the relations between human right and wrong. These ideas, combined in the unity of consciousness, constitute in their totality the ideal personality. This ideal consists, therefore, of a number of model "pictures of the will," which possess an absolute value and are independent of all desires. If they not only appear isolatedly in a human being, but permeate every state of his mind and heart, if they determine his guiding principles and the actions that proceed from them, then he is an embodiment of the ideal personality. Then the same man of character is to be recognized in every outward manifestation, and in all the walks of life. Wherever this constant harmony of the individual with the totality of ethical ideas appears, we speak of "moral strength of character." Wherever the intellectual life of man develops to a strong personal character in which the rational, the noble, the beautiful, and the moral—in general the logical, esthetic, and moral activity—triumphs over the merely mechanical processes in the human soul, then the highest and most significant stage of human educability is revealed.

If Kant and Herbart are right in claiming that the

will is the proper object of all ethical valuation, it certainly follows that *the ethical culture of the will must be regarded as the highest purpose of education.* If one aims to cultivate a good, constant will in the pupil, the absolute value of the educational end which he has in view cannot be questioned. This aim is revealed to us, furthermore, by an idealistic ethics which in general presents the highest necessary and universal purpose that should actuate human beings. It also furnishes theoretical pedagogics with its highest point of view in considering the question of the pupil's destiny. From the empirical idea of education we had already determined that a permanent form must be created in the inner life of the pupil; we now know upon the grounds of ethics what the nature of this mental form shall be. We can, therefore, place the following proposition at the head of our final conclusions: The educator should *so* educate his pupil that his future personality will be in keeping with the *ideal* human personality.

The *aim* of moral training then is nothing less than to make the ideas of the right and the good, in all their sharpness and purity, the proper objects of the will, and to render the real inmost content of the character, the essence of the personality, capable of self-determination in accordance with these ideas and without regard to any other possible purposes. But the aim of education appears to be reached when the personality is constantly intent upon bringing its actual volition into correspondence with the ideal activity of the will, when it uninterruptedly inspects its own volitional acts for the purpose of determining whether they were made to accord with the moral ideas out of pure love for morality, and whether as much morality was always willed and practised as the ideals demanded or permitted.

Hence the question of the *unity* of the educational aim is to be answered by referring to the ethical ideal of human personality that should be attained in the pupil. The doctrine of moral personality is the doctrine of the education of man within human society.

Every individual, whom the systematic efforts of the educator have brought near to the ideal of personality, who has learned to recognize the practical ethical ideas as the standards that should determine his inclinations and his actions, will be able with this preparation to participate best in bringing about the realization of the moral aims that are to be attained by the broader circles of society. Thus equipped he will take part most energetically in the moral elevation of human society, so that the demands of morality rather than the maxims of wisdom shall be recognized.

The child that has been educated in accordance with ethical standards, upon entering the circle of adult life, will of course often find himself at variance with the views which prevail there; for the motives of the larger or smaller circles of society are only too often determined not by ideal, but by very material points of view. But is it to be regarded as a disadvantage if the pupil meets such egoistical tendencies with the power of a better insight, and the courage of better convictions? How is society to be led to higher aims otherwise than by the gradual increase of the number of individuals who do not bend and become subservient to the dominant tendencies of the mass without further thought, but who, on the contrary, seek to suppress them whenever they rest upon immoral motives? He who takes the actual moral status of society as a model upon which to construct his educational ideal, will have to include in the bargain a great deal that is immoral beside the moral, for the existing moral condition of a people only signifies a certain temporary stage of development that is constantly changing. He who seeks absolute standards may, indeed, regard the moral status of society from a descriptive point of view; he may explain it and define it in all its phases, but he can only make use of it as a foundation upon which to demonstrate the necessity of higher standards and ideals that are independent of all fluctuations. These ideals, that are valid for both individual and society, furnish the absolute standards as opposed to the relative standards that have developed in the existing custom.

Everything depends upon whether one is convinced that the human race may be led up to higher aims. He who will do this must not place these aims too low. However flatteringly lesser aims, such as usefulness in human society, happiness, etc., recommend themselves to the great mass, moral elasticity will disappear if an ideal does not prevail that is ardently grasped by all, and which both the individual and the entire body of society should strive to attain with the application of all their energies and means. Society would then find itself dissolved into a mass of egoists, striving to overreach one another in the mutual contest, and seeking gratification as the highest aim of earthly life. The harmonizing centre for both the individual and society can only consist in the struggle after a common supreme aim which all recognize as the true purpose; otherwise moral torpidness will render both the individual and society incapable of all higher inspiration, and cut off all possibility of cultivating pure moral characters and noble, morally elevated communities.

(a) *Methodology.*

AFTER an educational aim of absolute value has been established and placed at the head of the entire system, our attention is next to be directed to the possibility of realizing this aim.

In fact, one of the first thoughts which occurs to us in this connection is that the belief in a moral ordering of the world vouches for the possibility of building moral character; but if on the other hand this belief is confirmed by a scientific foundation, if the possibility of influencing the youthful mind is psychologically demonstrated, the activity of the educator should, without doubt, gain greater stability and inherent certainty.

But the question as to the *possibility* of *improvement* does not depend alone upon the investigation of the human mind, but also directly upon the view of the world that has been developed by the individual or by some social body. If the crude forms of a false determinism exclude the fundamental pedagogical conception of the educability of the child, or if certain philosophical systems cannot support this conception without contradicting their own principles (as, for example, the systems of non-determinism which declare the will to be free in the sense that it is able to pursue a course which is in direct opposition to determining causes), the incompatibility of such views with pedagogical views is very apparent. If the possibility of a casual relation between the educator and the educated is entirely excluded, if the intellectual states of the pupil are regarded as either permanently determined from the beginning, or voluntarily changeable at any moment, education must appear as an impossibility and every attempt to educate as vain.

The opposite extreme finds expression in the words of Fichte: "If you would have any influence over man you must do more than merely talk to him, you must make him—make him so that it is impossible for him to will otherwise than you wish him to will." This reminds us of the view of Helvetius who ascribed to education an unbounded power over the pupil. According to his theory the pupil is entirely the product of the effects which education produces upon him. Even his volition, according to Helvetius, is entirely determined by it. Therefore, if education is active in the right way, the pupil *must* become whatever it aims to make of him. It would be fortunate for the educator if this were true, if he could assure himself that the soul of the pupil is a *tabula rasa* upon which he might write whatever his highest educational ideal demands, or if he could fashion it as easily as soft wax can be moulded in the hands of the sculptor. But the old saying: "Non ex quovis ligno fit Mercurius" would be sufficient to shake his confidence. Experience could give him still further warning and prevent him from thus overestimating the power of education.

However, it is without doubt to be preferred that the educator overestimate his power over the pupil than underestimate it. But in considering the possibility, extent and limit of education, he will always be inclined to shift hither and thither, preferring now this view, now that, as long as he does not appeal to *psychology* for information upon the fundamental question that is of importance to education, namely, the question concerning the intellectual constitution or the mental capacities of man. Of course he cannot expect a concordant answer from all psychologists; and in view of the obscurity which still prevails in this sphere, the different views as to the nature of the human soul and the extraordinary difficulty with which the empirical method of investigation meets, an absolutely indubitable explanation can hardly be expected. On the other hand the educator may rely upon a psychology that does not contradict empirical facts, but which demonstrates the possibility of influencing the formation of the youthful mind so plainly that he can establish his methods with confidence and expect success.

Let us now ask: what ways and means are offered the educator for advancing the pupil toward the supreme end of education? The answer usually comprehends two means, *training* and *instruction*. This distinction results naturally. The characteristic feature of instruction lies in the fact that teacher and pupil are engaged in common upon a third object while training deals directly with the pupil.[1] To the latter, therefore, has been ascribed the task of directly influencing the pupil on the side of the formation of character. Training educates the pupil to fear God, to obey and to speak the truth; it accustoms him to reserve his power and to practice self-denial. It is said that the strongest motives that actuate the will arise from love and desire; hence the observation, direction, and animation of the child's inclinations belong to the most important offices of the educator. The child is also dependent upon example in the development and purification of his feelings. The early habituation to a fixed order of life, to a regulated activity, vouchsafes for advancement and abundant blessings; here again the personal example of the teacher exerts a deep influence. In this manner a foundation of common views and moral convictions is imperceptibly laid, not by means of doctrines or ideas, but by means of the life itself and the personal intercourse between the teacher and the pupil. Accordingly the personality of the educator proves to be the most effective element in the moral training of the youth. By this same means also Plato solved the much discussed question of the educability of the youth thus, "Virtue can only be taught by virtue, in that the living exemplification of it awakens love and

---

[1] "Unterricht" and "Zucht" correspond very closely to the English terms, "Instruction" and "Training." It is well to bear in mind that a sharp distinction is made in the use of the German terms, "Erziehung," "Unterricht," "Zucht" and "Regierung," a distinction which of course must here be transferred to the corresponding English terms, Education,

the desire to emulate." If one were to ascribe everything to personal influence, however, he would have to sketch an ideal picture of the educator and perfect a catechism of directions as to how the teacher must be constituted in order to do justice to his high office. In fact not a few pedagogical works contain delineations of this kind, which hold before the educator, as it were, a sort of mirror in order that he may recognize of what he stands in need and what he must acquire in order to be able to discharge the duties of his calling.

Wherever this conception predominates and everything is left to the direct personal influence of the educator upon the pupil, it is self-evident that the second mentioned means of education—instruction—will remain in the background. Apart from the religious instruction, which by virtue of its very content is expected to exert an influence upon the will and disposition of the pupil, the different subjects of instruction pursue an independent end, namely, the accumulation of a definite amount of knowledge and facility, in order that the pupil may be able to provide for himself in the future. This last view corresponds to a widespread conception among families. How often the teacher is regarded not as an educator,

---

Instruction, Training, Government. The latter therefore should always be understood in the sense indicated by the text. (See also footnote, page 23.) "Zucht" has recently been rendered "Discipline"; although there can be little objection to the term philologically, its use in this sense is likely to create confusion owing to the fact that the German writers distinguish sharply between "Disciplin" and "Zucht." In either language "Discipline" is far too ambiguous.—*T's.*

but merely as a school-keeper. How often the notion is directly expressed: We—that is the parents, the families—provide for the education; you—that is the teachers, the schools—provide for the instruction. Family and school, training and instruction, according to this view, appear to be entirely disconnected factors, each one of which pursues its own independent task.

But such a conception is untenable from the standpoint of scientific pedagogics; for how can instruction be regarded as a means for the attainment of the supreme end of education if it serves no other purpose than that of preparing the child for usefulness in life? If this is the only business of instruction one does not need to trouble himself at all as to whether it will make others better or worse. In this case, that schoolmaster will be in the greatest demand who can place the scholar most surely and pleasantly in possession of the desired attainments. But such instruction does not accord with the conception of education. It has no connection whatever with moral training. This connection can only be brought about by placing the two means of education in relation to the supreme educational end. If one makes preparation for usefulness in life, *i.e.* utility, the purpose of instruction, he places the utilitarian principle on the same level with the ethical; that which has a relative value is placed beside that which has an absolute value. All development of mental power and facility in acquisition, every accomplishment according to their very nature, can enter just as well into the service of immorality as of morality. In the second case one must attribute a certain value to the instruction that developed these facilities; in the first case it must be denied. Hence, if one were to cultivate a knowledge of the useful and the power to apply it merely for their own sake, he would always be uncertain as to whether he served a worthy or objectionable end. We are, therefore, compelled to subordinate the aim of instruction to the supreme aim of education as required by ethics, and thus to place *instruction* by the side of *training* as an equally qualified factor.

Education and instruction must both make it their chief aim gradually to develop a system of ethical maxims in the pupil. These ethical maxims should comprehend the entire volitional activity, and be united and apperceived by certain chief universal principles, just as the individual concept is embraced and apperceived by the general concept. When this is the case the inner life of man receives that uniform stamp which we distinguish as a moral-religious character. In such a character one circle of thought is the supreme law-giver. This is the moral-religious circle of thought which asserts itself not only now and then on especially ceremonial occasions, but everywhere and at all times, which, as an invisible, apperceiving force, guides the will, the inclinations, and the actions.

In conclusion, we may sum up the means of education in the following outline:—

METHODOLOGY.

1. Theory of Guidance.
   (*Hodegetics.*)

   (*a*) Theory of Moral Training.
   (*b*) Theory of Government.

2. Theory of Instruction.
   (*Didactics.*)

   (*a*) General Didactics.
   (*b*) Special Didactics.

We turn next to the theory of instruction.

THE THEORY OF INSTRUCTION.

This subject sub-divides into two departments—General and Special Didactics.

General Didactics treats of:—

1. The aim of instruction in general.
2. The choice,
3. The arrangement (connection),
4. The treatment,

of the material for instruction.

Special Didactics treats of:—

1. The aim of the separate branches of instruction in their relation to the general aim of instruction.
2. The choice,
3. The arrangement (connection),
4. The treatment,

of the material for instruction in each single branch.

I. GENERAL DIDACTICS.

1. *The Aim of Instruction.*

According to Kant, the normal education of man should not begin directly with the improvement of the morals but with the metamorphosis of the sentiments and with the *foundation* of the character. Herbart, who attaches the chief importance to the development of the circle of thought, agrees with this view. And why should instruction not educate, since all wishes, desires, purposes, and resolutions proceed from the circle of thought,—in fact, were thoughts originally,—and since, furthermore, their energy is entirely dependent upon the help or hinderance which they experience among the other thoughts?

But if the formation of moral character, the cultivation of virtue, is to be placed as the aim at the head of the educational system, how is the aim of instruction to be formulated?

If it is true that the worth of man is founded not upon his knowledge, but upon his will, all learning must bear some relation to the end of education so that it shall be of some value to the future character of the pupil, in so far as his will is elevated, invigorated, and rendered efficient. Accordingly, all knowledge and power that are imparted by an educative instruction (*i.e.* instruction that makes for character),[1] must at the same time, directly or indirectly, serve the formation of the moral religious character.

The aim of instruction, accordingly, coincides directly with the aim of the formation of character.

But in order that the educator may see how this is possible, how the will may be influenced by instruction, psychology must give some more exact information as to the nature and origin of the *will*. It must be shown under what conditions the activity of the will is developed from the circle of thought. The educator aims to form the pupil's circle of thought by

---

[1] "Erziehender Unterricht" (educative instruction) is a specifically pedagogical expression belonging to the Herbartian system. It cannot be better defined than as "instruction that makes for character." See De Garmo, *The Herbartian System of Ped.* (ii.) in the *Educational Review*, vol. i, No. 3, N. Y.—*T.'s.*

means of instruction, in order thus to get control of the will, *i.e.* in order to give it a moral tendency as prescribed by the educational aim. It must be shown, therefore, how this is possible. This is the task of the following brief outlines.

There are *three chief forms of the psychical life*, representation,[1] feeling (the emotional life), and aspiration or desire. These are class conceptions under which the various phenomena of the psychical life may be comprehended conveniently and synoptically. They designate neither three souls, three faculties, nor three isolated powers of the soul.

The representations constitute the elements of the psychical life. Feelings and desires are special modifications that result from the conjunction of certain representations in consciousness. Feelings and desires are not independent entities that exist apart from the representations or ideas. The ideas, feelings, and desires of a human being are very closely connected. Especially is there no volition independent of psychical representation, *i.e.* external to the mass of ideas or external to knowing. It is true that we find ideas in the inner life with which no feelings, no desires are associated; but we never find feelings and desires that do not stand in connection with certain ideas or sensations, although the latter may be more or less obscure. Separated from all ideas and conceived of as isolated, the will is nothing. The activity of the will is rooted in and proceeds from the mass of thoughts. Volition is a condition into which the

---

[1] Representation ("Vorstellen") includes all the psychical states that *represent* to the consciousness, as it were, some content, such as a sensation, perception, idea, concept, etc.—*T's.*

ideas are brought by some definite cause or occasion. If this is true, instruction may also acquire power; it also influences the will by the development and manipulation of the mass of ideas. Thus the aim of education coincides, harmonizes with the aim of instruction; the one proceeds from the other. Instruction must so form the circle of thought that volitional activity will develop from it.

But how does this take place? Not all knowledge produces volition. The latter is a mental activity of a peculiar kind, a new starting-point in the development of the activity of the soul. Volition, it is true, has its roots in the circle of thought, but it only proceeds from the latter under certain conditions. What are these conditions?

Knowledge is frequently only a dormant store of facts that are in themselves apathetic; in other words, it is merely a fund of finished, quite clear ideas. As long as this is the case no volitional activity can be developed from it. If volition is to proceed from this knowledge it cannot remain such an inanimate fund; on the contrary, mere knowing must be effected in a twofold way; the knowledge must penetrate into the sphere of the disposition, (1) as something that is felt, (2) as something enlivening. When this is the case, then that mental condition, which we call *interest*, is present.

The *aim of instruction* may accordingly be defined as the training of the circle of thought by means of the interest, so as to render it capable of volition. (Knowledge—interest—volition.) The interest should not be one-sided; otherwise one-sidedness of the personality ensues, a condition that is at variance with genuine morality. The latter demands that a strong personal character shall cultivate a many-sided interest. This *many-sidedness* comprises six classes of interests which may be divided into two groups of three each. We arrive at this classification by means of the following considerations:—

The human intellect places itself, so to speak, before the objects with which it is occupied and views them as something *foreign* to itself; or it grasps them just as it conceives of itself, as members of the world, of its world, and thus stands in *mutual intercourse* with them. To the mind, accordingly, they are either objects of *knowledge* or *intercourse*.

In the first case we have to deal in part with the conception and observation of objects in their manifoldness (empirical interest), in part with the knowledge of their mutual dependency and with a reflective examination of the same (speculative interest), in part with a judgment of them in accordance with the standards of the good and beautiful (esthetic interest). In the second case we have to do with the *mutual intercourse* or *association* either with animate beings or with beings which we conceive of as possessed of souls. We either devote ourselves to them as individual beings with whom we are in harmony, in whose weal and woe we participate, and in whose conditions we place ourselves (sympathetic interest), or we turn our interest to the entire body and share and live through its fortunes (social interest). But the feeling of dependence, of impotency, which we have when placed face to face with destiny and the Incomprehensible, the longing for a balancing of the relations between the actual and the ideal, produce the religious interest.

THE THEORY OF INSTRUCTION. 91

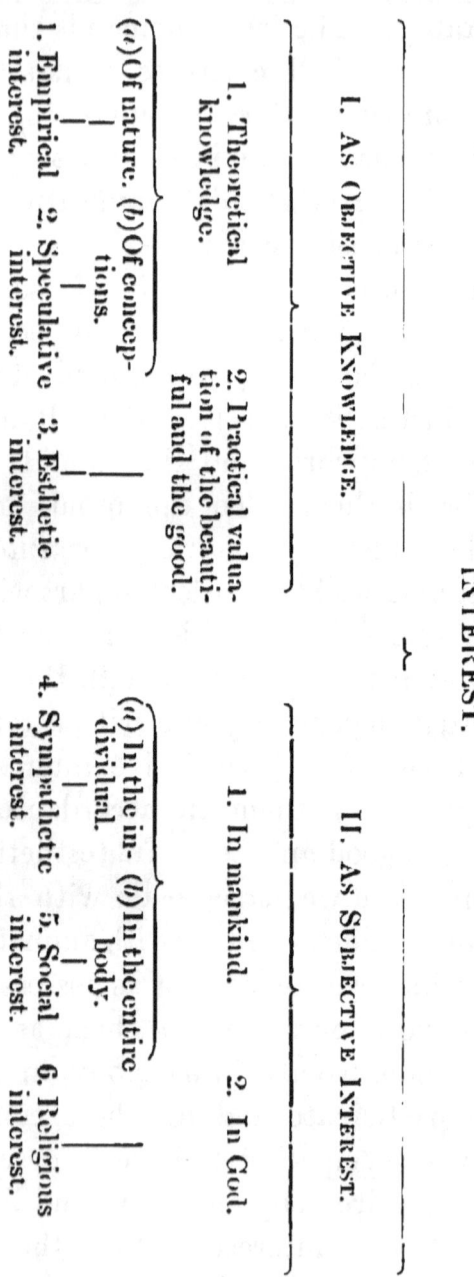

INTEREST.

I. As Objective Knowledge.
1. Theoretical knowledge.
  2. Practical valuation of the beautiful and the good.
    (a) Of nature. 1. Empirical interest.
    (b) Of conceptions. 2. Speculative interest.
    3. Esthetic interest.

II. As Subjective Interest.
1. In mankind.
2. In God.
    (a) In the individual. 4. Sympathetic interest.
    (b) In the entire body. 5. Social interest.
    6. Religious interest.

The aim of instruction, therefore, is *not* the production of a many-sided knowledge, but of a many-sided interest. At the same time those facts of knowledge and those facilities of which the pupil has future need in the execution and furtherance of the practical purposes of his life, fall to him of themselves; yet *utilitarian considerations* should never stand in the foreground. The genuine, direct interest should never be repressed by an indirect interest. At the same time, the instruction must take care that the idea of the *good* retain command in the inner life of the pupil, that it retain its prominence in the midst of the other contents of consciousness. Instruction, therefore, must give the will the moral tendency; the scholar should learn to discriminate between possessions according to their true value; he should see that it is just the sensual pleasures and possessions that are most sought, but of the least value; he should learn to regard *mental* possessions as of the most worth, and to recognize that the want of that most valuable of all possessions—a good conscience—destroys the value of all others.

Hence the effect of instruction is *truly educative* when it

1. Produces a deeply-rooted, many-sided, permanent interest in the pupil;

2. When it insures the necessary energy for the moral-religious interest, and at the same time

3. Vouches for the unity of the consciousness as the basis for the development of a strong personal character.

This is the highest aim of instruction when conceived of as in the service of the formation of character.[1]

---

[1] An excellent and somewhat more extensive, theoretical and practical presentation of the subject of "Interest" may be found in C. A. M'Murry's *General Method*, chap. iii.

2. *The means by which the Aim of Instruction is to be realized.*

(a) *The Selection of the Subject-matter of Instruction.*

Without doubt the next most important question for him who aims to educate through instruction, *i.e.* to create an interest, is what material or what ideas shall be introduced to the youthful mind? The great question of the *selection of subject-matter* takes a prominent place in didactic considerations. In undertaking the selection of subject-matter we must proceed from our aim, the awakening of the many-sided interest, in order to obtain a scientifically established series. The first maxim may be formulated as follows: Only that should be subject-matter of instruction which is able to awaken and chain the interest of the scholars. Only such material should be chosen as must necessarily awaken a spontaneous, permanent interest in every child of normal, mental endowments. The interest only has a real value for education when it arises spontaneously in the pupil, accompanies him through his school life as a permanent mental activity, and still inspires him after his school years as a vital power that will always augment. But the preliminary, psychological condition that must characterize all ideas capable of producing interest upon entering the circle of thought, is similarity; there must be a close affinity between them and other ideas that are already possessed and that are expecting them, as it were. This condition requires the most exact consideration of each particular stage of apperception. This is a demand which Goethe expressed in the words: "One could be genuinely 'esthetic-didactic' if he could pass with his scholars before all that is worth feeling, or if he could bring it before them exactly at the moment in which it culminates and when they are most highly sensitive."

Let us compare this with another passage from Goethe: "The human mind receives nothing which does not suit it." Here we are directed to select the mental nourishment exactly in accordance with the existing capacity of the child's mind to receive and digest it—a fundamental principle that has long since been applied in the sphere of physical training.

As the first condition for the selection of material, we may grant the following proposition: Only that material which corresponds to the child's power of comprehension, *i.e.* to his particular stage of apperception, will be able to excite a deeply-rooted lasting interest in him. But this provision alone does not suffice; for one might suppose that in order to select suitable material he has but to collect from the entire literature of the world, from the cultural attainments which the various peoples of the earth have stored up, all that is exactly suited to the needs of an educative instruction. Accordingly, if one is merely intent upon selecting that which is adapted to the child's power of comprehension, Greek and Roman ingredients would be found beside Egyptian and Chinese, modern elements beside the antique, and national beside the foreign. Apart from the fact that this method of procedure would result in a remarkably miscellaneous collection, it would also work in direct opposition to a *second* principle that is included in the conception of the moral character. At some future time the pupil must be able to be active in life; he must participate self-actively in the tasks which the present places upon him. *This present*, in fact, is not that of any people whatsoever; it is the present of *his* people —at least as long as mankind is still divided into a number of individually different nations. But in order to be able to take an independent part in the modern activity of his people, he must first learn to grasp this present itself properly in all its tendencies. Hence arises the second *requirement* for the educator: Observe the present cultural standpoint of the people and seek to have a right understanding of it in all its phases developed in the pupil, in order that he may learn to find for himself that sphere of labour which he intends to enter as a moral personality.

This demand would also be quite right if the first-mentioned requirement that has just been established, and which enjoins that the child's power of comprehension be taken into consideration, did not run directly in opposition to it. For the present of a cultivated people—and only such a people can be taken into account here—presents such complicated relations that it would be utterly absurd to attempt to nourish the child's intellect upon it. One would very soon find that the interest of the child can never develop on material which contains too many difficulties, because of a complicateness that the work of centuries has wrought. This would endanger the result of instruction from the beginning, and work in direct opposition to its aim.

Let us now recollect that the present rests upon

the past; that he who desires to effect some lasting good for the future must join it on to the present, which is to be understood alone through the past.

These considerations turn us back from the complicated relations of the present that are more difficult to grasp, to past times that are more simple, more easily understood and, at the same time, more easily adaptable to the conceptive power of the young mind. From this standpoint the material for the educative instruction should be sought in *the development of the national culture*, which is to be followed in its chief eras. It should be presented from its very beginnings, *i.e.* from the point at which a constant progress is apparent, up to the present. This principle, which agreeably to its content we may call the principle of *historical culture*, also harmonizes, as we shall see at once, with the *psychological* requirement that the subject-matter in each case correspond to the child's stage of apperception. The *material* and the *formal* points of view coincide. A people does not stand at once upon a definite height of culture; centuries of zealous and unwearied labour are necessary before the height can be reached. It must climb up from lower to ever higher stages; it must pass from simpler to ever more complicated relations in order to satisfy the bent for improvement and the realization of the kingdom of God upon earth. And the individual, the same as the people, rises in his development from lower to ever higher stages, from simpler to ever richer mental contents, if only his ideal tendency be not smothered by material sensuality or by the feeling that he has already attained a fine height. Thus we must accept on the one hand *historical*, on the other hand *indi-*

vidual, stages of development or apperception. It is obvious that if the two series—the historical, with its various cultural materials, and the personal, with its manifold ideas, wishes, and desires—can be brought successfully and accurately into harmony with each other, one can undoubtedly get control of the scholar's interest, because by this means the psychological conditions would be best established. The development of the *individual* is nourished on the development of the *whole*. Whenever a subject can claim the height of interest, it enters into the circle of thought; being expected, it is welcome, and the direct interest makes its appearance provided the educator possesses the necessary art of instruction. As a matter of course, the most careful selection of material is useless when there is a lack of skill. But this careful selection of subject-matter will give the educator unsuspected assistance as soon as he understands it. How often the teacher toils over less worthy material, and the interest refuses to appear in the youthful soul. Conversely, what a relief for the teacher whenever the material with which he is occupied is congenial to the child's mind, when it enters just at the moment it is actually expected and is greeted as a welcome guest in whom one becomes more and more interested.

We find that this idea of the analogy between the individual and general development of humanity is a common possession of the best and most noted intellects. It appears, for example, in the works of the literary heroes Lessing, Herder, Goethe and Schiller; with the philosophers Kant, Fichte, Schelling, Hegel, Comte; with the theologians Clement of Alexandria,

Augustine, Schleiermacher ; with the Darwinists Huxley and Spencer; with the classical philologists F. A. Wolf, Niethammer, Dissen, Lübker ; with th pedagogs Rousseau, Pestalozzi, Froebel, Diesterweg, Herbart, Ziller and others.

From the large number of voices let us select but two, Goethe and Kant. The former said : " Although the world in general advances, the youth must always start again from the beginning and, as an individual, traverse the epochs of the world's culture." The latter points out that the education of the individual should imitate the culture of mankind in general, as developed in its various generations.

This thought of Kant's and Goethe's only needs to be cleared from its hyperbolic presentation and brought into harmony with the conditions of instruction. One cannot undertake to impart a world culture, for no one knows where it is to be had, but only to provide wholesome and digestible nourishment for the pupil's interest by introducing him to the development of the *national* life. Hence we must undertake an analysis of the *national circle of thought;* this alone is the determinative factor in the organization of the material for an educative instruction. The series of subject-matter for the educative instruction is to be drawn first of all from the development of the national culture. At the same time the opportunity will offer itself for many a glance at the history of other nations in so far as their fortunes are connected with those of the fatherland.

The cream of these periods of development, as it is preserved in science and art, constitutes the subject-matter of an educative instruction. The chief content of these historical series must now be condensed, concentrated, embraced under typical, but at the same time classical forms, and offered as nourishment for the development of the youthful mind. In this connection it is well to note that these types are not to be presented in broken, disconnected pieces or bits, but in *large connected masses*. Moral power is the effect of large, unbroken masses of thought; in these alone can a strong interest be developed. A great deal will have been gained as soon as the attention of the educator has been drawn from the vague and scanty materials of instruction to the great classical materials, and his eye been opened to their buoyant didactic power.

This will have been accomplished as soon as he conforms to a scheme for the selection of material, which, upon the ground of the preceding investigations, we may sum up in the following propositions. The choice of material for the educative instruction presupposes a twofold preliminary work.

1. The *psychological work*. Its task is to establish the stages of development of the individual mind from both the theoretical and the practical standpoints.

2. The *historical philosophical work*. Its task is clearly to define and sum up the chief eras in the historical development of the people.

These two preliminary tasks are then succeeded by

3. The *work of the pedagog*. Both series—the individual and the general—must be brought into harmony with one another. The individual mind must traverse the entire historical development in a rapid, concentrated manner by means of the material

which the national growth has produced. The individual must thus be prepared, as a moral character, to comprehend at some future time the height which the present has reached, and to take part independently in its tasks, however modest his position in life.

In this way the educator must endeavour to establish a complete regularity in the succession of the subject-matter which corresponds to all requirements. This natural and unbroken succession of material is the most radical means for rendering instruction properly efficient, and for freeing the curriculum from all caprice in the choice of matter.

At the same time the educator must always keep the following propositions in mind:—

1. The development of the national culture can only produce permanent interest in the developing human being, in so far as it is presented and grasped in the light of the ethical judgment. For this reason we choose the chronological ascent from the older and simpler to the newer, more complicated stages and relations.

2. Classical presentations that are accessible to the youth must form the basis of these studies. Periods that no master described, whose spirit no poet breathed, are of little value to education (Herbart). Only classical presentations invite the pupil to return to the treasures that never cease to reward him, and that fill him with interest and inspiration. It is only through such sources that the past speaks to the present with a clear, distinct voice.

3. Large, entire and connected portions of a subject are alone able to arouse a sufficiently deep interest in

the youthful mind, to keep it permanently on the alert, and thus to effect the formation of character.

We may close this subject with a brief summary. The developing human being can only take an interest in and comprehend the *growth* of his people; the pupil can only be brought gradually to an understanding of the present and its tasks, and his own method of thought be established at the same time, by successive absorption in the chief stages of the national progress of the past, in so far as they are at hand in classical presentations. This *ascending series of the chief historical stages* can rely upon a corresponding series of *stages in the development of the inner life of the pupil*, and hence upon his deepest interest.

It should, therefore, be the first aim of instruction to make a selection of material in accordance with the historical principle (stages of culture).[1]

(b) *The Co-ordination of Material for Instruction. The Connection of the Branches of Instruction. Concentration.*

Following the principle that has just been established for the selection of matter, a thorough analysis of the entire material for instruction furnishes us with several series which run co-ordinately and present the different phases of the national educational activity. Thus we have the religious and moral series of development, the series of profane history, the esthetic or artistic series, the linguistic series, the series of the natural sciences and geography,

---

[1] See also C. A. McMurry's *General Method*, chap. iv., and the supplementary remarks beginning on page 116 of this work.—*T's.*

the mathematical series, etc. It should be the office of these series to present the chief eras in the development of the single sciences as it has taken place within the nation. Accordingly, as many separate branches would be subjects of instruction as there are phases in the cultural activity of the nation.

Without doubt an enormous amount of the most diverse ideas have been stored up in these series; they constitute a heterogeneous mass that is brought from the market of life where it is distributed among many forces, into the laboratory of the school in a concentrated form. Will not the school succumb under the burden?

This question has very often been answered in the affirmative, but no one has been able to suggest how the evil can be met; or, if any plan was advanced, its demands still remained very general. Let us consider the following statements for example: "All conceivable expedients should be devised in order that time and energy may be economized and an intensity in the results of instruction be attained, through unity in the foundations, association of related materials and the combination of mutually complementary elements. When one finds in certain courses of study, history of the Middle Ages, reading from Herodotus, geography of America, and German literature since Lessing, side by side at the same time, he ought to be glad if, in accordance with the old custom, the youth does not trouble itself much about some of these favours, but, withdrawing its interest from them, devotes its energies to the independent cultivation of some special portion of the field of instruction." This is undoubtedly true; but it is hardly to be designated as a healthy condition. On the contrary, it is our duty to convert the *confusa varietas lectionum* into an *ordinata varietas*.

But how is this to be done? The history of didactics shows various attempts to apply a *concentration* of instruction,—for we are accustomed to designate the connection of the branches of instruction by this name. All of these attempts, however, have thus far been able to accomplish so little of universal validity, that the name "concentration" has been brought into no slight miscredit. Hence the *confusa varietas lectionum* is still the rule in the majority of our schools; but it is nevertheless by no means right. Such a conglomeration of subjects in the plan of instruction places the most insurmountable obstacles in the way of educative instruction. The task of the educator, briefly expressed, must be to convert this aggregate into a systematic plan of instruction. Two requirements urge him to the attempt: (1) an ethical, (2) a psychological.

The ethical requirement demands that the educator endeavour to collect the forces of the pupil, in order that they shall not be trifled away, but through their concentration result in an energetic and powerful activity. No moral character is conceivable without such concentration of forces. But if the pupil is to undertake the concentration of his power, we must provide, above all, that the circle of thought be as compact as possible, and not disconnected.

Psychology teaches in what manner the unity of the person develops. The person, *i.e.* the ego, is not an original, but a developing entity; hence, it is also a changeable being. The ego is a psychical phenomenon, namely, the becoming conscious of a lively and constant interaction within the more or less invisible complex of ideas; in other words, it is the consciousness of the inter-relation of all our ideas, and the psychical conditions that arise from them. The inherent ground for the inter-relation of all our manifold ideas, for their synthesis, as it were, at one point, the ego-idea, must be sought in the simplicity of the soul, which strives to unite all psychical contents that are not separated by antithetical and arrestive influences. The soul is self-active as a concentrative force in opposition to the manifoldness of impressions and influences that are furnished by experience and intercourse.

But the constructive activity of the youthful mind is overestimated, if one assumes that it would of itself establish the connections between the manifold circles of ideas. In fact, even in adult persons the concentrative power of the soul is often not strong enough to produce unity of consciousness as the basis for a uniform personal activity. Where a large number of entirely different and disconnected ideas have been developed, real unity of the person based upon the unity of the consciousness is impossible. Without this unity, however, a character is inconceivable. Unity of consciousness is the primitive foundation of character. Instruction, therefore, must be directed towards establishing this foundation; it must further the concentrative power of the soul by means of its various arrangements. It should never place obstacles in the way, an error which occurs whenever heterogeneous ideas are brought into the consciousness at the same time and then quietly left to their fate. Hence, after a regular succession of subject-matter has been established in accordance with the historical stages of culture, the next task is to provide an equally well-arranged co-ordination of the various materials for instruction.

The thought may now occur to us to lighten this task of co-ordination by abandoning the cultivation of certain circles of ideas from the beginning. But it must also be possible to establish a harmonious connection between the unity of the person and the plurality of the branches of instruction even when all the necessary educational elements are retained. If one were to strike out a certain number of instruments from a symphony, the work of art would be destroyed. The efficiency of instruction will be impaired in the same way if certain essential educational elements are not included in the curriculum.

These thoughts recall certain words from the encyclopedia of Stoy.[1] Here it reads on page 11, "Instruction can hardly be thought of more pertinently than when compared to a symphony in which, in fact, at different times, single voices take the lead with the 'motivo,' then retire and make place for others, and finally all together unite harmoniously in one grand stream."

We can only agree with this simile in part; for in the educative school the ideas should, by all means, be combined into a unity that contains no contradictions. The disharmonies that must occur—as for example, when the teacher of natural science sneers

---

[1] Stoy, *Encyklopädie der Pädagogik.*--T's.

at religious ideas, and, conversely, when the teacher of religion abhors the investigations of natural science as the work of the devil—such disharmonies should not by any means be brought into the youthful mind, for the reason that they destroy the unity of the circle of thought. Such work runs in direct opposition to the purposes of educative instruction. Thus far the comparison is suitable. But it is incorrect that the separate branches of instruction in the educative school should alternately stand in the foreground, in the same manner that the various voices in the symphony precede one another with the theme. The maxim, "One thing after another," is, in general, wrong, because it is not compatible with the principles of educative instruction.[1]

An examination of the educational value of the single branches shows at once that those studies are to be given the preference in the instruction of the school, which work directly for the attainment of the educational aim, and which, by virtue of the content they convey to the pupil, are able to meet the demand for a valuable circle of thought in which the moral-religious interests predominate.

---

[1] This statement is not intended by the author to signify that all possible branches of study are to be pursued synchronically. It by no means precludes the possibility of introducing one language, for example, after another, or of arranging the elementary science-instruction so that the various sciences are treated at the most favourable moments as regards the season of the year, their dependence upon one another, etc. Neither does it preclude the gradual introduction of studies in proportion to the growing capacity of the child. It is to be understood rather as referring to the general classes of material,—historical branches, language, art, science, mathematics, etc.—*T's.*

If one keeps the supreme purpose of education in mind, the branches of learning may be easily and distinctly ranked in accordance with their pedagogical importance.

This conclusion is by no means intended to express an undervaluation of any of the single sciences; but it by all means aims at a correct proportionment of the amount which they may contribute to the formation of the youthful mind and character. Above all, the predominence of linguistic studies is thus also reduced to the proper limit, and the fiction of "formal education,"[1] which still haunts many minds, but which rests upon just as crude a conception of the intellectual life as the hypothesis of materialism, is removed, or, at least, placed within bounds. Occupation with the symbols of ideas (language) is certainly of undoubted value for all future use of such symbols (for example, in the acquirement of another language), but indeed for nothing else. Furthermore, the acknowledgment of this fact is at present constantly spreading, so that one may assume that the true significance of the so-called "formal education" will soon be placed everywhere in the right light. None of the branches of instruction can be regarded as a universal means, the intense pursuit of which could develop the formal power for mastering all other series of material. On the contrary, they should all be taken equally into consideration, if the genuine, many-sidedness of interest is to be obtained. The only question is, how shall this be accomplished? The problem which is to be solved may be briefly stated once more in the following sentences:—

---

[1] See page 42, footnote.

The centre of the educator's activity is the developing personality of the pupil to which the manifold interests must always be referred. Now, how is the concentration of the branches of instruction to be subordinated to *this* concentration, whose centre is the developing character of the pupil.

We have already spoken of those branches of instruction that introduce the "leading motivo" ("Leitmotif") of education. They comprise the material that is directed especially toward the training of the disposition. These take the most prominent position, since it is their purpose to place a weighty and connected mass of thoughts and inclinations in the mind and heart. These ideas should be of such weight, and have so many points of contact with every new thought which may appear, that nothing can pass by, no new combination of thoughts can take place without reckoning with this centre of the circle of thought.

THE FIRST GROUP OF BRANCHES.

1. The material for the training of the disposition[1] is drawn from three series; (1) from the religious material (from biblical and ecclesiastical history); (2) from profane history; (3) from literature. The latter, however, will only appear as a special, independent branch in the higher educational schools. Between these three series there must be a reciprocal relation, an inner connection. This connection is at once

---

[1] Gesinnungsstoff.

vouched for by the arrangement of the material in accordance with the historical development of culture in so far as it may be followed in its religious, social and ethical phases. Thus the historical principle of culture and the psychological principle coincide.

2. The above-mentioned material for the training of the disposition is supplemented by the branches of art; for example, drawing and singing, both of which are directed chiefly to the nurture of the esthetic interest. The close relationship that exists between the ethical and the esthetical, insures these branches a position next to those that train the disposition; their content is naturally and closely related to that of the historical branches from which they receive the necessary hints as to the selection and arrangement of material.

3. To this group belong also the languages, which constitute the formal side of the historical material. All historical records, in fact the cultural development of a people, is stored up chiefly in its great literary monuments. From these we draw the artistic aim, the ability to make the linguistic expression the interpreter of the thoughts of the inner life. At the same time also the interest is awakened in the language itself, as a very characteristic and significant creation of man. In this sense the teaching of language appears as a branch of the humanistic instruction, *i.e.* as a branch of the historical instruction. But in the educative school the language is only a *means* to an end, not the reverse. Grammatical instruction can claim no independent position as do the philological sciences in the university.

This closes the first group of branches, which we

may designate as the historical group. It possesses a certain ascendency; for wherever we have to deal with the formation of an ethical personality, a circle of ideas capable of supporting a moral character must occupy the central place in the entire world of thought. If it is true that the precedence is due to the ethical ideas as the forces which determine the personality of man, material which directly serves in the production of these ideas can also claim the precedence.

THE SECOND GROUP OF BRANCHES.

The second *group* of branches of instruction includes the natural sciences. An analysis of the elements of culture shows us that the work of mankind is directed on the one hand to the ideal sphere— *i.e.* to religion, mental sciences and art—on the other hand to the investigation of *nature*. Accordingly these two large groups of material may be summed up under the phrases—life of nature and life of mankind.

We arrive at a similar result by analyzing the child's circle of thought, which, as already emphasized, develops partly through experience, partly through intercourse. The child draws experiences[1] from the

---

[1] The author here makes an important distinction between "Erfahrung" and "Umgang," for the sake of brevity and clearness, which must also be transferred to the corresponding English words, "experience" and "intercourse." The distinction originated with Herbart.—*T's.*

objects of its environment. It enjoys intercourse with its parents, brothers and sisters, and playmates. Experience refers to the domain of nature; intercourse to that of human life. Instruction supplements both of these sources and is also divided into two chief lines; it enlarges the *actual* human intercourse by means of an *ideal* intercourse with the men of fiction and history; it enlarges the experience of the pupil in the domain of nature by leading him to make observations, collections, experiments, descriptions, etc., and at the same time works over this experience in its formal phase as regards form and number.

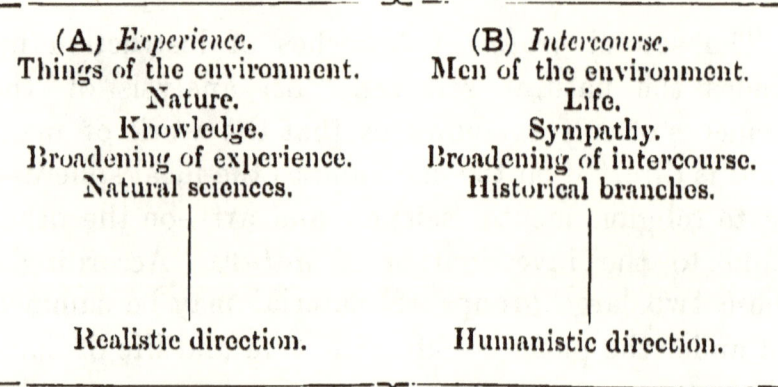

THE CIRCLE OF THOUGHT.

(A) *Experience.*
Things of the environment.
Nature.
Knowledge.
Broadening of experience.
Natural sciences.

Realistic direction.

(B) *Intercourse.*
Men of the environment.
Life.
Sympathy.
Broadening of intercourse.
Historical branches.

Humanistic direction.

The two directions fuse in the general education furnished in the educative schools.

To the second group, which we designate as the natural science group, belong the natural sciences in the more restricted sense, geography and finally mathematics, the branch that represents the formal side of science.

Thus we have obtained a twofold division of the branches of instruction and the circle of thought. If one were to content himself with this result, the question of concentration would have to accept only a partial solution; one would abandon the uniform effect of the branches of instruction and therewith also the production of a uniform circle of thought. The pupil would constantly incline now more to the one, now more to the other side, according to the fluctuations of the interest But nothing is more dangerous for the character than to be constantly thrown about hither and thither from one circle of thought to another without being able to sum them up in a higher reflection. A theory of the course of instruction which contents itself with this twofold division would give clear evidence of its own incapacity to effect a uniform organization of the branches of instruction.

Therefore one is compelled to investigate the further question as to how the second group of subjects is to be arranged with reference to the first group so as to produce a higher, more complete unity. *Geography,* as an associative science, is the first to offer its services in answering this question. It is the natural companion of the instruction in history, in that it undertakes to treat the countries in the succession in which they have appeared to the intellectual sphere of mankind. Hence, it presents, in a condensed form, the history of discoveries. The connection of the *branches of natural* science with the historical series proves to be more difficult. In this case the investigations may often be connected unconstrainedly with the treatment of geographical objects, in order to furnish the latter the necessary supplementary support. Thus, to cite an example, the investigation of the Alpine flora and fauna could be placed beside the geographical treatment of the Alps. On the other hand, we should also consider that the life in Nature may also be viewed from the standpoint of human purposes. The will places itself in relation to things of Nature in order to bring them into the service of man. Human activity experiences limitations from two sides; it is limited (1) by the ethical ideas, and (2) by the nature of things. This obligation to the moral ideas limits the *purposes* of action; restriction by the nature of things limits the *means* of action. On the other hand, these two spheres contain aids to human activity as well as limitations. In the education of the will both must be brought to the pupil's consciousness; he must acquire (1) an understanding of those limitations and aids that are based upon the ethical ideas, (2) an understanding of the limitations and aids that depend upon the relations of things in Nature.

The first is the office of the instruction that especially trains the disposition. The latter is the office of instruction in natural sciences. Thus both series, both the chief groups, unite in that higher reflection at which the education of the disposition aims. Both series, taken together, furnish the materials for the pictures of culture which should be viewed both from the standpoint of their time and that of the pupil, and should chain his interest as a constant ascending series.

Thus we have sketched in the rough the plan of concentration for the curriculum of an educative instruction.

In this plan all the elements are represented that should be considered in the formation of the curriculum:—

1. The ultimate moral and religious purpose.
2. The harmonious psychological and historical gradation of the instruction.
3. The correlation of the various materials of instruction.

Organized in accordance with this programme, instruction may become an unbroken educational force, comparable to organic matter. And yet plans of instruction are constantly being created by the mere artless collection of the series of material; curricula are constantly being prepared in which merely the matter to be treated is considered, but not the question as to what materials will be co-ordinated in the application of the plan, nor how they may be connected. A sort of educational atomism is apparent here, which has taken hold of the work of instruction and thinks it can produce an organic structure by the mere accumulation and piling up of material, a living being by the mere mechanical co-ordination of forces. In contrast with this tendency we may cite the thought of Plato's, that the branches of learning should always be viewed in their connection and understood according to their relationship.

The following summary may serve to render this relationship clear once more.

EDUCATIVE INSTRUCTION.

Two Spheres of Material.

(A) Life of Man.
Historical-Humanistic Branches.

I. Instruction for Training the Disposition.
1. Biblical and Ecclesiastical History.
2. Profane History.
3. Literature.

II. Art-Instruction.
1. Drawing.
2. Modelling.
3. Singing.

III. Language-Instruction.
1. Mother Tongue.
2. Foreign Languages.

(B) Life of Nature.
Branches of Natural Science.

I. Geography. II. Natural Sciences. III. Mathematics.
(For the Cultivation of Bodily Activity, Turning, Games, etc.)

With the above may be compared the classifications given by DÖRPFELD and ZILLER.

DÖRPFELD.

(A) Branches of Learning.
Nature ; Human Life ; God.
Knowledge of Nature, History, Geography, Religion.

(B) Mother Tongue.
Speaking.
Reading.
Writing.

(C) The Separate Facilities.
Arithmetic.
Drawing.
Singing.
(Turning).

1. Group.	2. Group.	3. Group.
1. Historical Series.	1. Languages.	1. Geography.
2. Natural Science.	2. Mathematics.	2. Turning.
	(Drawing).	3. Technical Occupations.
		4. Singing.

Supplementary remarks on the application of the preceding sections (a) and (b).[2]

Our system has thus far fixed upon its educational aim (character-building) and the aim of its instruction (the many-sided interest), and has entered upon the consideration of the means of instruction. Here the Herbartian school distinguishes three great principles—the *historical stages of culture, concentration,* and the *formal steps of in-*

---

[1] It is very apparent that the first of these three classifications is based upon a clear principle, and one that may be derived directly from Herbart's own views. The second and third do not seem to have sought a logical principle of classification, but merely to have adopted an arbitrary grouping that would serve practical purposes. There can be no doubt that Herbart always had two main groups in view—the historical and the scientific. See also C. A. McMurry's *General Method,* chap. ii.—*T"s.*

[2] The object of these supplementary remarks is to give some conception of the application of ideas that, especially in their practical phases, are more or less new to the English and American teacher. The intention, therefore, is only to supply a guide to the general application; proposals for any single case can only be made where all the circumstances are known. The special applications, therefore, would necessarily differ among themselves according to their different circumstances. Wherever specific propositions are made, they are intended to be suggestive rather than determinative.—*V. L.*

struction. The first two of these three principles, with which we are concerned here, have been theoretically and psychologically established in the preceding pages. It is now our task to inquire somewhat more minutely into their general practical application, for the question now occurs to us at once: Can these principles be applied? One can only obtain an answer to this question (1) by referring to attempts already made to apply these principles and summing up their results, (2) by testing their applicability for himself. A conclusive and convincing answer, either *pro* or *con*, cannot be had until both means have been employed. The following statements are based upon curricula[1] arranged in accordance with the aforesaid principles, and upon extended observations of their successful, practical application.

In our further investigations we shall endeavour to keep in mind the aim both of education and instruction as already established. We have already seen (page 99) that there are three tasks to be performed in laying out the course of study:—(1) The stages of development in the child's mind are to be determined, (2) the national stages of development, the national eras, are to be determined, and (3) the latter are to be placed, so far as possible, parallel to, and in harmony with, the former. As a result of these preliminary works, the course of study already referred to, which is arranged only for the eight years of the people's school, presents the following summary of material for the historical instruction :— [2]

---

[1] *Theorie und Praxis des Volksschulunterrichts*, by Prof. Dr. W. Rein, A. Pickel, and E. Scheller, Leipzig.

[2] It is almost impossible to produce an adequate translation of the German term, "Gesinnungsunterricht," which is used here. "Historical instruction" has, therefore, been used above, and must be understood in the more restricted sense.

1. School Year.			Märchen.
2. ,, ,,			Robinson.
		Sacred Series.	*Profane Series.*
3. ,, ,,		Patriarchs and Moses.	Thüringer Tales.
4. ,, ,,		Judges and Kings.	Nibelungen Tales.
5. ,, ,,	⎫ Life of Christ.	⎧ Christianizing.
6. ,, ,,	⎭	⎩ Kaiser-period.
7. ,, ,,		Paul.	Reformation.
8. ,, ,,		Luther. Catechism.	Nationalization.

As may be seen, the historical instruction bifurcates after the first two years into a sacred and profane series; but the division is merely external. A glance at the corresponding materials *for each year* (which are here highly generalized) in the two series, shows that they harmonize internally with remarkable accuracy. The unity is preserved. This arrangement of material refers only to the time at which the various periods are methodically treated. It by no means excludes the possibility of the child's hearing of Christ in the first four years, for example; numerous opportunities are at hand (Christmas, Sunday, devotions, etc.) to provide for this necessary part of the earliest training. Here we have to do merely with the gradual general development of the child's conceptions of sacred and profane events for the sake of their uniform and harmonious effect upon his character. Neither is all that may be included under each one of these general headings undertaken. Only enough is brought before the child in well-chosen "pictures of the will," to present the period in its essential characteristic features. Here the culture and good common sense of the teacher are in demand. Let us notice further that certain general features of development are apparent, showing that this is not merely a chance parallelism. For example, a glance at the industrial phases of national life presented in these two historical series reveals the following typical stages:—1,

Hunter's life; 2, Nomadic life; grazing is a new occupation of man; lower animal life enters into the service of man; 3, Agricultural life; 4, Development of retail trade and small industries; 5, Development of wholesale trade, foreign commerce, and great industries; growth of great cities. The lines cannot be sharply drawn between these several stages; natural development seldom displays marked signs of transition. We simply find the development of certain industrial phases predominant at certain periods in the history of a nation. A similar comparison may be applied to the cultural development.

In the same way we find certain psychological changes that correspond in general to the psychical development of the child. In the first six years of its life the child's psychical development consists chiefly in conscious reception and reproduction; it is occupied with its numberless sense-perceptions of the outer world and learns its mother tongue. Comparison, thought, are as yet primitive. This period includes also the years of the kindergarten. At the time the child enters school, his imagination is beginning to show signs of lively development; he longs for fairy tales; he is like the people that has risen above the stage of mere sensual impression, and is beginning to develop a national imagination, and hence a culture. Its first literary treasures will be highly imaginative. His will, as yet, experiences no severe conflicts. He still relies entirely upon his childish trust. At a later stage the mechanical memory appears in its most marked phase; the childish imagination continues active. As in the first school years, he is still eager for wondrous tales, and his mental possessions continue to increase. But he often finds his will coming into unpleasant conflict with other wills both in his games and in his work. He must learn the bitter lesson of subjugation to the will of the whole.

A further stage finds the understanding struggling to

rise, to gain control over the mass of material in possession of the mechanical memory. There is a strong desire to create something with one's own hands. Independence is beginning to develop, for the child is getting control over its will. There is still often a lack of perseverance in completing the tasks that have been independently and voluntarily undertaken.

The closing stage of childhood is characterized by rapid strides toward the predominance of the understanding. New things are viewed in the light of old mental possessions. The ability to judge correctly is greater. The will is still further under control. It determines the actions of the individual in accordance with his moral ideas, his principles, his conscience.

Thus we have characterized in very rough, brief outlines the development of the child in his first fourteen years of life. Let us repeat again that neither these stages nor their individual features are fixed. They vary in different natures; they frequently overlap, and the transition from one stage to another is of course imperceptible. So far as an approximate estimate can be made, each one of the four stages beginning with the sixth school year may be regarded as corresponding to two of the eight school years. We have simply characterized the child in general at several different times in its life for the purpose of comparing his development with that of a people. A glance in comparison at the above series of historical material shows an undoubted analogy with the development of the child, and demonstrates that the material thus chosen is suitable for the child's mind. Let us not make the mistake, however, of expecting too much from this comparison, this analogy. It is sufficient to guide us; it is all that could be expected; but it is not complete, for if this were possible all individuality whatever would be removed. What, then, is the general result? We have a series of material for use in the historical instruction that corresponds to mental development of the child in general, that is suited to his powers at each stage, and that gives him a survey of the historical development of his people, culminating at the time he enters a maturer life.

The first two years constitute a sort of preliminary course, in which the imaginative element predominates. The following six years present, in general, a gradual national development from superstition, ignorance and unruly will-power to enlightenment, understanding and the joint-will of a good government. This development is analogous to that just traced in the child. The entire series contains rich ethical material, whose proper treatment (see page 135) cannot fail to develop a moral content in the child's mind. Can anyone doubt that this arrangement, which provides for a gradual ethical, social, and national development of the child, extending through his entire school life in one unbroken stream, could be otherwise than effective? Does it not bear a great contrast to the usual arrangement of the curriculum, in which the guiding principles have seemed to be merely to find material for each grade that was easy enough for the child at that age, and to satisfy the demands of both tradition and the popular novelties?

What effect this principle of succession in the curriculum will have upon other branches we shall consider shortly. Let us next consider some of the most noteworthy objections that have been made to the above principle.

1. Sticklers for chronology will object that the chronological order is not preserved. But what teacher of history that is master and not slave of his subject was ever able to preserve the chronological order? Nor is this a prerequisite. Let us remember that that which is psychologically near to the child is not always chronologically near him. The psychologically near must have the preference. Again, the historical development is by no means disturbed if the changes in chronological order do not extend over too large

periods. This development would be violated by a change in the chronological order of distinct, purely historical periods, but not in the order of events that have a common character, and that belong to the same epoch.

2. It must be acknowledged that the principle of historical development is directly opposed to what has been termed the principle of "concentric circles," which is to be distinguished sharply from "concentric instruction," or "concentration" in the Herbartian sense. The principle of concentric circles has been very influential in the past. It aims to give the child the simplest elements of all branches in the first school years, and then to repeat the work on a larger, maturer scale in the last years. Sometimes the same subject is treated from its foundation up in this manner three times. Behold the "primary geography," the "intermediate geography," and the "higher geography"! This method of procedure is incompatible with the historical stages. It has but one psychological fact upon which it is based, a fact that by no means renders it imperative. It is an attempt to take the steady development of the child into consideration. The child's powers grow; his unfolding understanding is capable of seeing facts in a newer and broader light. How can this be possible if he passes over a subject, or a part of a subject, but once and only in his earlier years? We at once answer, this is a problem that depends upon the art of the teacher. The Herbartian pedagogics is, in general, opposed to giving the child a certain mental content, and then allowing it to rest. It aims to keep the entire mental content alive by producing constant relations between the old and the new. In fact, it has a specific term for old ideas, *viz.* "apperceiving concepts." These familiar mental possessions are constantly in demand when the child is acquiring new circles of thought. But that is not the only result of their constant activity. They themselves steadily grow and deepen in the light of the

newer material, and with the child's unfolding understanding.[1] Again, practice supplies the necessary support to the memory. Thus the principle of historical stages meets in a much more satisfactory way the demand made upon the curriculum by the child's mental development. The material for each grade is treated in a manner suited to the mental status of the pupil. The old is broadened, deepened, and renewed in the light of the new. At the same time, the treatment of the subject-matter is reinforced in this work of maturing old circles of thought, by the course of study itself, for the latter presents a regular series of material, whose content becomes more mature as the mental horizon of the child broadens. But what can we advance from our own standpoint against the so-called principles of concentric circles?

1. One of its well-known effects is the dampening of the interest. Too often it requires the pupil to repeat processes, with which he is already familiar, for the sake of the mere repetition.

2. Again, it constantly breaks up old series of ideas and requires the formation of new, a revolutionary process that is more or less disturbing to the psychical life. So far as possible the work of instruction should be so arranged as to produce little waste in the formation of fixed series of ideas. It is very evident that the principle of concentric circles (which, happily, is rapidly losing its power) is also the cause of a great waste of time. It is a principle which we cannot afford to make the determinative factor in the formation of the curriculum, especially at a time when numberless new demands, the out-growths of a higher civilization, are being constantly placed upon the schools.

3. The attempt to give the child an epitome or general survey of each branch in his earlier years inevitably results in feeding him upon dry, uncomprehended generalities. It

[1] Compare the supplementary remark on the *Formal Steps*, page 146.

cuts off the possibility of cultivating careful observation and perception in the very years when the child is most receptive for the individual impressions of his environment, and when he should be laying up a store of particular facts from which to draw careful and more mature generalizations.

A fourth objection will be noticed when we come to consider the subject of concentration.

Thus far we have only considered the historical instruction of a curriculum arranged for the common schools of the country in which this movement originated. We now ask, are these principles applicable elsewhere, *i.e.* are they general principles? Leaving the sacred series of the historical instruction as it stands (for, in case religious instruction were imparted in the schools, it would remain essentially the same, with slight changes, of course, in the last year as regards the reformation), let us attempt to make the application elsewhere, in a general way, for the sake of illustration. We are not making a study of any national pedagogical principles, but of principles that are capable of application anywhere, if one but takes the different circumstances duly into consideration. As this volume is addressed to English readers, we cannot do better, perhaps, than to view the principles briefly in the light of their possible application in the schools of English-speaking nations. We shall only attempt this in the most general manner, for as has already been emphasized, the curriculum should receive a different stamp as to its particulars, according to the location of the school.

The two years' preliminary course could remain the same. The choice of tales (fables) for the first year would depend largely upon the locality in which the children lived. They should, so far as possible, be peculiar to his people, or better, to his state or community. They should be classical, and their contents should not be purely and wildly imaginative, but ethically valuable as well. *Robinson Crusoe* is a common literary treasure of the English-speaking nations. But its educational value was first recognized by Rousseau, a Frenchman, and systematically applied by Ziller, a German Herbartian. Anyone who has read Robinson (and who has not?) and who will reflect for a moment upon the vast amount of elementary ideas upon geography, zoology, botany, art, society, etc., that it contains, will see at once that this is just the material for the second year, when these same elementary ideas are beginning to unfold somewhat more definitely in the child. The most recent experiments with this material depart somewhat from Defoe's narrative, in that after Robinson reaches the island, he is made to accomplish everything he can for himself with the raw materials of Nature before he discovers the ship. His rude clothes, weapons, pottery, cave, and labouring implements present to the child the first step in the history of culture and art. The comparison that follows when he discovers the ship, and has the gun, the powder, the axe, saw, and hammer, the cloth and the books of civilization at his command, is one that arouses the deepest and most permanent interest, and gives the child a valuable mental content.

This preliminary work might be followed in English schools by some such material as this:[1] 3rd year, *Old English Legends*, characteristic of the earliest days, which may be chosen without a strict regard to chronology; they would, above all, include the legends of *King Arthur and the Round Table, Robin Hood*, etc. 4th and 5th years, *The Settlement of England*, as presented in its legends (See Freeman's *Old English History*), *The Anglo-Saxon Forefathers, the Danes*, and *The Christianization of England* (Egbert, Alfred, Canute, Augustine, Paullinus, Dunstan, etc). 6th year, *Great English Kings, from William the Conqueror to the War of the Roses*. 7th year,

---

[1] For suggestions here I am indebted to J. J. Findlay, formerly headmaster of Wesley College in Sheffield.

Renaissance, Reformation, Age of Discovery to 1763. 8th year, *Development of Modern England.*[1]

The arrangement of the historical series presents greater difficulties for the American school, for the reason that the national development of the United States can only be correctly regarded as a continuance of certain tendencies more or less manifest in England since the time of the Magna Charta. But the difficulty is not entirely insurmountable. All of the material necessary is at hand. After the preliminary course of two years, the child has already heard of the savage in Robinson. The transition is natural to a few Indian legends. In them he learns of the original inhabitants of his country. Soon the Indian meets the white man, and the child is introduced to a series of pioneer stories, beginning with those first which lie closest to his circle of thought.[2] This material would occupy the 3rd and 4th years. The question is then brought to the child's mind,—whence these white men, whose coming has brought such changes to the land and its former inhabitants? The answer to this question must be sought in the history of discovery and exploration,—a step backward chronologically, but a step forward to the child. Then follows the history of settlement and colonial history, two more school years (5 and 6) being required for the whole. The last two years would then be devoted to the Revolution and the Constitutional period.[3]

---

[1] Among the abundance of literature that may be used as reading matter in concentration upon the historical material, may be mentioned *Readings from English History*, by J. R. Green, M.A., LL.D., and *Historical Ballads*, by Charlotte M. Yonge.

[2] *Pioneer History Stories for the Third and Fourth Grades*, by C. A. McMurry.

[3] Since writing the above I have read the propositions of Dr. Charles A. McMurry, in his *General Method*, which coincide in the main with my suggestions. The latter were originally sketched somewhat more fully with the kind assistance of my countryman, A. C. Rishel of Chicago. It seems to me that use should by all means

The above suggestions are sufficient to give the reader some idea of a general application. He can compare them with that which precedes, and enter into the particulars as regards material for himself.

It will be asked, does this not introduce the child to history too early? We answer, No. Experience has demonstrated that there is no branch of instruction capable of arousing a deeper or more lasting interest in the child, when properly treated, than history. When the historical series is adapted to the child's stage of apperception from the first year and presents a gradual development, there is no danger that the child will not be able to grasp or be attracted by the events of history, providing they are presented with a fair degree of skill; he begins in any case with the simpler relations and advances to the more complicated.

Concentration.—What effect will this arrangement of the historical instruction have upon the formation of the curriculum as regards the other branches of instruction? We can answer this question by reference to the principle of concentration, which has already been established theoretically. Let us consider it briefly in its practical phases. It has been very aptly said [1] that "the psychological basis for the principle of concentration is to be found in the activity of apperception," and that on this account concentration in the curriculum and in the instruction is at the same time most efficient aid in obtaining the child's permanent and penetrating interest. We have already heard that "the developing personality of the pupil is a centre to which manifold interests must always be referred." This can mean nothing less than that the mind is active as an apperceiving

---

be made of the pure Indian legends, and that this material, leading to the life of the pioneer with whom the Indian comes in contact, is fitted for the 3rd school year.

[1] See W. T. Harris in *Public School Journal*, Bloomington, Ill., vol. xi., Nos. 2 and 3.

force; it recognizes, identifies, assimilates as a unit, a centre. The pedagogical principle, therefore, that is based on this psychical activity, we call concentration. According to this principle, the various branches should be united to a whole in the curriculum; according to it the instruction should be carried on.

For the sake of clearness one may distinguish two forms of concentration: (1) Concentration in the curriculum and (2) concentration in instruction. Both forms of concentration take into consideration,—(*a*) the previous instruction and (*b*) the life, environment, and experiences outside of the school.

We make use of past instruction in concentration when we compare Robinson with Boone, Africa with South America, when we solve one geometrical problem with the assistance of others previously solved; we make use of the child's environment in concentration when we read, "The snow had begun in the gloaming, etc.," at some appropriate time after a snowfall, not in July, when we present a rural, descriptive, heroic, or historical poem to the child, just at the moment when he can see and feel its fitness (*Authors' Birthdays*), and when we draw upon his knowledge of the surrounding country, of its points of historical, industrial or geographical interest for apperceiving concepts.

Let us consider first concentration in the curriculum. The objection has often been made that if the historical stages are to be valid, all branches should be arranged accordingly, and that this would necessitate the teaching of alchemy before chemistry, astrology before astronomy, etc. This would be very true if we had to do with history in these cases. But we have not. The principle of the historical stages is applicable to all of the historical branches without difficulty. As regards other branches we are only concerned with truth as we see it to-day. If this truth bears a relation to the child's life it is capable of being brought into harmony with the historical instruction of the school. The historical material is intended not only to impart knowledge, but also, above all, to develop the child's character through his ideas. It therefore stands in close relation to the child's own personality all through the common school course. Hence it must form the centre of all instruction. To the historical series as a centre the other branches are to be referred. Their relations to the life and work of man must be made clear to the child. He must be conscious of the fact that all knowledge bears a very definite relation to man and his affairs. Here concentration enters the field. Let us not harbour the erroneous idea that the other branches are now to lose their identity, to become mere puppets in the hands of the historical instruction. By no means; each necessary branch will retain its distinctive character, receive its distinct portion of time in the daily plan, and be allowed to pursue its own specific aim, in so far as it serves and does not violate the supreme aim of education and instruction. Let us now take the separate branches in order, for the purpose of seeing how they may be concentrated. We begin with the historical branches. The historical series in the more restricted sense has already been discussed. After it has been laid out to suit the school and the circumstances the next branch to be considered would be—

Literature and *Reading.*—In the last few decades a great deal has been written for children in the English tongue. A number of writers have turned their attention to historical subjects and have produced much that should be turned to account in the school. Besides this newer material, the older classical literary treasures contain much that is within the grasp of the child, especially in the last school years. Thus, with the exception of the first two years, by a careful selection of material, the reading of the child can be made to bear upon his historical studies. Thus, too, his knowledge of the subject is enriched and very often his memory refreshed. In the first two years the child is occupied with the task of learning to read. Yet even here, as soon as a little facility has been attained, concentration can help him. The fairy tales, fables and Robinson can be had in sufficiently simple form. But we must not forget that the child is *experiencing* real life at the same time that he is *learning*. His holidays and national celebrations, the changes and events of nature, the events of his native place also furnish numerous occasions that should guide the teacher in bringing home to the child the circumstances which called forth some literary treasure.

Singing.—After considering the concentration of reading, it is not difficult to understand how singing is to be concentrated. Here, above all, the national songs come into requisition; their meaning should be made the more significant to the child through their relation to the historical material. As before, the environment of the child is another determinative factor in the selection of material. In all cases, as a matter of course, the child's facility, which is but a means to an end, must be taken into due consideration.

Drawing.—In the first school year the child begins to practice that form of drawing which the Germans so aptly designate as "Malen" or "Malendes Zeichnen." For want of a better term we may call it *rough sketching*. He depicts in the rough his conception of the object he sees. It is one of the tasks in which he is freest, in which he creates at will. This rough sketching is kept up throughout the entire course, gradually improving in character, and entering into the service of geography, science, mathematics, and even history. Its use is to bring the unfolding concepts of the child to light, where he can see them, as it were, to simplify the objects of perception, and to illustrate. In this phase, drawing is chiefly a concentrative means. But its sphere does not stop here. Early in the school course the child is introduced to exact drawing. Here teachers in the European States have a great advantage over those in America. The architectural structures that are to be found in almost every village and city of civilized Europe furnish the most abundant objective material from which to proceed. The churches, cloisters, public buildings, castles and palaces of Europe, even in a ruined state, contain all the artistic forms that can be found in any drawing course. In addition to this, the history of art is contained in them. The teacher can, with ease, so arrange the drawing lessons of the pupil that they present the development of art in its chief epochs, parallel to the epochs of history. At all events, where possible, the work should be started with the inspection of a work of architecture. A single church will furnish material enough for months of work. Thus, in two important lines, drawing may be made one of the most valuable and helpful concomitants of the historical instruction. What has been said of drawing is also true of modelling. The very best results of both are to be found in the esthetic culture of the child. This esthetic culture is only to be had by a study of the historical development of art, chiefly as displayed in the treasures of architecture. If a nation is too young to have passed through these stages itself, its modern structures and art treasures should be analyzed with a view to bringing out the original forms and styles upon which the whole is based.

Language.—We have already shown how literature and reading may be concentrated to the historical instruction. The further instruction in language has reference merely to facility in speaking and writing. A properly-directed historical instruction, beginning with the first and closing with the eighth school year, is the most important and effective means for developing facility in speaking. The material deals chiefly with narrative, which always gives the pupil less difficulty than almost any other form of discourse. The grammatical studies should be connected with the text that is placed in the hands of the pupil. The content of some literary selection forms the objective material for the child's grammatical perception. From it he derives his grammatical system. Work in composition should draw upon the different series of material; above all, let it beware of selecting its subjects at random from spheres that are entirely foreign both to the child's life and environment, and to his present and past instruction.

Geography should bear the closest possible relations to the historical instruction. The very nature of the subject facilitates concentration. The history of one's own nation not only treats of the one people, but constantly reveals points of contact with other lands. These points of contact give occasion for the geographical study of these countries. Nor need this principle of selection disturb the systematic development of the branch in the least. The points of contact are so numerous that the most suitable moment for introducing the child to each sphere can easily be found. When he hears of the ideas and deeds of Columbus, for example, he is at once interested in attaining a deeper insight into the mathematical relations of the earth. If his mind is at this time mature enough, this is the time to open the subject; if not, some other natural and suitable time may be chosen. It is also quite in keeping with the principle of concentration to postpone political geography until the last school years. At this time the child is occupied with modern history, and the opportunity is favourable for taking another view of the world in its political aspect. This is of especial importance to him as a future citizen. The development of the last century has brought his country more than ever in contact with the entire world. This contact reveals to him the true standing of his nation.

Mathematics and the Sciences.—These branches are more difficult to concentrate than those previously mentioned.

Still concentration is here possible and beneficial. A large share of the work of concentration is accomplished in the instruction, as we shall shortly demonstrate. Otherwise these branches are to be considered as the bearers of knowledge that enter into the service of man. This fact is brought to the pupil's consciousness by drawing upon the various, already concentrated series for the concrete material of mathematical problems, for example. If such a problem opens a "method-whole" the child understands its connection with life, and the demands of concentration are satisfied, the unity is preserved. In the same way some fact that has appeared in the historical series, or in one of the other series with which it is concentrated, gives the impulse for scientific investigations. Both mathematics and science, however, should find a centre for their work in the life and environment of the child, for here the objective material is found, upon which the entire instruction should be based.

Thus far, we have not prepared a curriculum of instruction, but have merely indicated how its historical centre might be selected and the plan of concentration applied. Let us now consider "concentration in instruction" in its broadest application. When the child enters upon a new subject, its connection with the whole should be made clear to him at once. In stating the aim of the lesson, for example, the teacher refers directly to the bond that unites the geographical study of a certain land with the historical work. In the majority of cases the wide-awake pupil is able to state the connection without assistance. In the same way a thousand lines may be drawn that show the complete interrelation of all the child's tasks. As soon as the bond is perceived, however, the subject of instruction pursues its own course. Furthermore, the teacher who is alive to the importance of concentration must be thoroughly acquainted with the environment and life of the child, and make a constant use of the objects that are known to the child wherever they will aid apperception. He also arranges his school-walks and journeys so that they will accord with and further the work of instruction He never forgets that the child has been acquiring facts of all kinds from the time of his birth, and that these facts constitute the apperceiving concepts for the new. Concentration furnishes a strong argument for advancing the teacher from grade to grade with his scholars. There can be no doubt that he is best fitted to teach the child who not only understands his nature in general, but also has an intimate knowledge of the specific contents of his mind.

In closing, let us consider for a moment some of the advantages which a course of study, arranged in accordance with these principles, offers in addition to those already discussed in preceding chapters. First, the curriculum is relieved of a great deal of pressure, due to the old habit of unnecessarily reviewing entire subjects merely for the sake of review. These principles provide for the refreshing of the old, but demand constant progress in instruction. This by no means excludes term or yearly reviews, but merely the old plan of elementary, intermediate, and higher courses in the same branch in the common school. But what is to become of the vast amount of work that has been devoted to the preparation of text-books on the old plan? We answer, if the teacher is master, and not slave of his textbook, they can still be serviceable to him. Upon what principle is the old system of five or six readers based, for example? What demands that the teacher shall slavishly drive his pupil through each reader from the beginning to end without regard to the fitness of the material, or to a suitable order? But, to follow out this example, these readers contain much valuable material; the teacher must follow a higher ideal and select the literature, not the book. This is true of any branch. Therefore, time is gained for the increasing demands which modern civilization places upon the school, by setting aside useless repetition. Again, one of the subordinate aims of education is to train patriotic citizens. The historical instruction, which forms the centre of the entire school life, is better able to satisfy this demand than any artificial means. This plan of instruction also constantly enlivens the interest of the child because it constantly fosters the acquisition of related knowledge.

The historical stages and concentration in their effect upon the course of study must appeal to those who prepare the latter. Concentration, however, can always be of use to the teacher in practice. He can only make use of the historical stages at present, in so far as they do not conflict with that which the present curriculum prescribes. The above illustrations will suffice to show how the application may be made in general; the individual application must be left to the reflection and study of the teacher.

Exhaustive data as to the application of the principles of concentration and the historical stages of culture for any other schools than those in which they were first applied and have been worked out in detail, cannot be given until the attempt has been made to apply them in other fields. It will not be necessary here to indicate how they may be, or have been, applied in the higher class of educative schools that prepare for the higher professional studies. If the child enters upon its classical and linguistic studies seasonably and before the years of childhood have been brought to a close, the history of general culture can be presented to him in the same way that the child of an eight-year common school passes through the history of his nation's culture.— *V. L.*

(c) *Treatment of the Subject-matter.*

After the proper material has been chosen and suitably arranged, the next task is to present it to the scholars, so that it shall become their permanent possession.

The systematic treatment of the subject of instruction is generally comprehended under the name of "*method*" in the more restricted sense of the word. The view of Herder, who said: "Every teacher must have his own method; he must have created it himself through his own intelligence, or it is of no advantage to him," is, in fact, widespread, but fundamentally false. A confusion of the concepts, method, and manner, lies at the basis of this proposition, for there can be only one method. As Comenius has already said: "There is but one natural method for all sciences, arts, and languages." This is true if we accept the hypothesis that the human soul works according to definite laws, if we grant the supposition that psychical processes conform to laws the same as physical. According to this supposition there can be but one natural method of instruction, *viz.* that which conforms exactly to the laws of the human mind and makes all its arrangements accordingly.

Therefore, he who is in possession of knowledge and insight into the laws of psychical life, can also obtain possession of the right method of instruction. Hence it follows that the natural method can only be regarded as an idea, as a goal that is placed before us; for who would boast that he possesses a psychological insight which spreads out before him the workings of the human mind as plainly as if they were the workings of an ingenious machine in a factory? "Vous voulez mécaniser l'éducation," said Glayre to Pestalozzi; and, as Pestalozzi himself said, "He hit the nail upon the head." Over-zealous disciples have boasted that Pestalozzi actually mechanised education, *i.e.* he understood the development of human nature in accordance with its organic laws, even in the entire range of its being, relations and activity, and constructed the educational machine and set it in action accordingly.

But this laudation of the Pestalozzian universal method not only resulted in subjecting the endeavours of Pestalozzi himself to the sharpest criticism, but the spirited disciples of naturalism in instruction were newly strengthened in their aversion to all methods. But the truth must, nevertheless, be advanced against these scorners of all method; even the most happily constituted nature, the teacher by divine grace, is not restricted nor rendered ineffective by the directions of method; on the contrary, his activity is promoted and insured of its effectiveness. But the objection that the one natural method has, in fact, not yet been found, and perhaps never will be found, within any imaginable time, may easily be removed by reference to the fact that the pedagogical labours of the past have produced results of great value to the work of instruction, which no teacher can neglect with impunity. No one will assume that the highest stage in the development of method has been reached thereby; everyone will admit that the newer directions signify only one step further on the way that leads to the highest goal, *viz.* the finding of the one natural method of teaching.

The latter, in as far as it is known at present, may be sketched in a few words.

We met with two sharply antithetical views as to the choice of material—formalism and idealism. The former inscribed so-called "formal education" on its banner. The material of instruction was only a means to an end, *viz.* the formation of the understanding. The latter insists upon a valuable content in the material and upon the education of the dispositions. There are also two sharply antithetical views as regards the methodical treatment of the subject-matter—(1) didactic materialism and (2) psychological realism. The former aims at the acquisition of as much knowledge as possible in the school, the latter at the methodical treatment of as much material as is thoroughly consistent with mental health.

Didactic materialism marks the lowest stage of method in instruction. The pupil is compelled, whether he will or not, to work his way into the subject. That which is required of the mental power of the adult is also simply demanded of the boy's brain. This is the conception that ruled throughout the entire Middle Ages. The method of procedure in instruction conformed exclusively to the nature of the object of instruction, not to the nature of the one learning. The first isolated efforts to develop the subject of method appeared with Ratich and Comenius, and were directed toward treating and presenting the material of instruction with some reference to the mind of the scholar. The eighteenth century, a veritable century of pedagogy, brought to light a series of pedagogical systems (as afterwards in philosophy) which attracted the attention of people in all stations of life, and permeated all literature. The first of these efforts went to the extreme in that their devotees (philanthropists) sought to shorten, sweeten, and flavour the work of learning. The chief endeavours of Pestalozzi and his disciples aimed to divide the subject of instruction in accordance with the needs of the pupil, and unfold and steel the power of the scholar on the material thus prepared. The movement which Pestalozzi started was so strong that it has made the following age what may be termed the age of so-called methods. The newer didactics seeks to remove this biased preference for method and to advance the development of the curriculum; hence it would also do justice to the single educational elements themselves, and attribute to them an inherent value

Recent didactics, however, has permitted an uncommon simplification to enter into the subject of method as compared with the constant desire and rage for methods that characterized former years. It has thoroughly cleared away everything that had falsely assumed the name of method, and has produced a theory which, in its simplicity and clearness, parallels the true work of art, whose naturalness and simplicity never lead one to suspect what pains and what application it has cost the producer. The so-called Socratic, rational, developing, catechetic, demonstrative, practical, mechanical methods, etc., have been cleared away. Whatever recommends itself in these conceptions as independent method, must now take a more modest and befitting rank as a didactic form subordinate to the whole; in fact, even those didactic forms which Herbart recognised as real methods, *viz.* the analytic and synthetic, must be combined to a systematic whole, or surrender their independence.

The great advantage of the newer methodics consists in the fact that theory has found the way for practice. Formerly, the great majority of teachers, even among Herbart's pupils, wondered at the network of abstract conceptions to be found in his *Allgemeine Pädagogik* without knowing what use to make of them. This apparent labyrinth of concepts was first transformed by Professor Ziller of Leipzig into a theory which can actually direct the practice of instruction in the right course by means of a series of practical and adaptable imperatives.

That the intellectual constitution of the pupil must be taken into consideration as the chief determinative factor in the treatment of the material has already been repeatedly emphasized; for one is led at once into darkness and error as soon as he ceases to deduce the principles upon which he bases his method from the psychical process in the soul of the child. But by following the directions which this process gives, he arrives at a definite articulation of the instruction which corresponds to the growing interest of the pupil. This necessity for a clear, definite articulation of the instruction, based upon psychological grounds, is aptly set forth in the familiar words of Quintilian: "Pour water rapidly into a vessel with a narrow neck, and little enters; pour slowly, and but little at a time, and the vessel is finally filled." The "how much at a time" would, in general, be difficult to determine, since the individuality of the pupil and the nature of the material must be consulted. If the educator, however, inspects the material that has been laid out for a longer period of time (and he must do this if he does not wish to be dependent upon chance), he must first consider the division and arrangement of these connected masses into smaller wholes, such as may be treated with the pupil in a complete normal process of abstraction. Such a portion we designate as a "method-whole"[1] or "method-unit."

After the method-wholes within a single branch of instruction have been fixed upon, the treatment of material then begins by presenting the aim[2] of the lesson; it is intended to give the thoughts of the pupil a definite tendency, and to arouse his expectation. It puts the pupil in mind of known things and processes, and opens to him at the same time a vision of something that is new, and as yet unknown. The statement of the aim of the lesson, therefore, calls old ideas into consciousness, whose activity is indispensable for the understanding and assimilation of the new, and directs the will of the pupil to the solution of a problem to which he must devote all his energies. But it is of great value to the educative influence of the instruction, if the pupil always knows what he is after, if his intellectual activity assumes from the beginning that impress of *work* (in that it strives to attain a definite aim) which distinguishes it plainly from any definite *play*. The pupil engages in play as an end in itself; but he does not work for the sake of working nor to fill up the time, but in the hope of solving a problem that attracts and chains his attention. The statement of the aim of a lesson has achieved its purpose, if it has led the pupil from the beginning to regard the task that is to be accomplished as important. The formulation of the aim is, there-

---

[1] See De Garmo's *Essentials of Method*, p. 75-77.
[2] To be distinguished, of course, from aim of instruction.

fore, neither an entirely easy task nor a matter of indifference.

If the aim of the lesson has been rightly put, it produces a flood of thoughts in the pupil at once. This is above all essential, if one expects to produce clear percepts from which to deduce accurate notions. In fact, the process of learning may be summed up in these two activities. From the percept to the concept or notion—this is the truth which Pestalozzi as clearly recognized and expressed as Kant, who said: "Perceptions without general notions are blind; general notions without perceptions are empty." The percept is a product of both external and internal observation; the notion which cannot arise directly from the senses is a product of thought. Therefore the educator must provide himself with definite answers to the two following questions:—

1. How do we obtain clear, distinct percepts?
2. How do we obtain clear, distinct notions?

Psychology alone gives an answer. It teaches us that the first question finds its solution in the process of apperception, the second in the process of abstraction.

METHOD OF TEACHING.

Percept.	Concept or Notion.
Apperception.	Abstraction.
(Lange, "Über Apperzeption.")[1]	(Dörpfeld, "Denken und Gedächtnis.")

Abstraction is only possible upon the ground of

---

[1] See Bibliographies.

experience which constantly presents to us material in the form of single, entirely individual, concrete facts. The broader the concrete substratum, the more successful will be the formation of notions. Very often one must content himself with psychical or individual concepts, where there were not sufficient number of examples for perception at hand to introduce a normal process of abstraction. The formation of logical concepts is in general a very slow and gradual process, which never fully comes to a close during a lifetime.

Now, wherever notions are to be formed, a natural method of instruction always conforms to this normal process. In so far as the method of teaching succeeds in imitating the normal process of concept-formation, so far is it healthy, simple, and natural. In so far as instruction departs from this process, it becomes involved in unnaturalness, subtilities and abnormal methods of procedure. Wherever a method proceeds in accordance with the nature of the human mind, genuine interest will appear spontaneously and faithfully accompany and further the instruction; wherever the educator does not trouble himself about the psychological conditions of learning, he will always need artificial aids to incite the attention and be a match for the pupil.

If the scholar works under pressure, if he feels learning to be a burden, there can be no mental growth. It is otherwise where free interest prevails; then everything goes easily, teacher and pupils work with a will and experience sincere joy in their labour. This is only possible, however, by means of an exact psychical adaptation and adjustment of the method to the youthful moods and ideas. Nature makes no leaps; neither should an instruction that proceeds in accordance with Nature.

Wherever the psychical conditions, individual perceptions and general notions, are kept in view, wherever one proceeds in accordance with the growth and condensation of concepts from percepts, the method of instruction will consist of two successive stages. Within a method-whole, some concrete material of knowledge, be it external or internal, will always be presented for the perception of the pupil; then follows the transformation of this material into concepts. Both processes subdivide into two steps: the process of apperception into (1) the preparation of necessary, related, already known material, and (2) the presentation of the new ideas; the process of abstraction into (1) the comparison of all known cases, and (2) the extraction of the essential and the generally valid. A final step then provides for the necessary application of the knowledge that it may become ability, power, which is always at command. Accordingly the "theory of the formal steps of instruction" distinguishes five steps, as shown by the following synopsis:—

THE THEORY OF INSTRUCTION.

FORMAL STEPS.

I. Dörpfeld and Wiget.	II. Herbart and Ziller.	III. Rein.
1. Perception. { (a) Percept. (b) Notion. } Apperception.		1. Preparation.
	(a) Introduction.	2. Presentation.
	(b) Perception.	
2. Thought. { (a) Comparison. } Abstraction.		3. Association.
	{ (a) Analysis. (b) Synthesis. }	
3. Application. (Power.) { (b) Condensation. }	1. Clearness.	4. Condensation.
	2. Association.	
	3. System.	5. Application.
	4. Method (Function).	

With the above may be compared the designations given to the "formal steps" by the following American writers.

I. De Garmo.[1]	C. A. McMurry.[2]
I. Apperception. (Sense-perception.) (Concrete illustration.) { 1. Preparation—Analysis. 2. Presentation—Synthesis.	I. Presentation. { 1. Preparation. 2. Presentation. 3. Association and Comparison.
II. Abstraction. { 3. Comparing and uniting, or, Induction, Association (Socratic). 4. Formulation of Notional—Deduction; from which we descend again to particulars.	II. Elaboration. { 4. Generalization or Abstraction.
III. From Knowing to Doing—Application.	5. Practical Application

[1] *Essentials of Method*, and *Language-Work below the High School—Primary Language-Work.*
[2] *General Method*, chap. viii.

K

The above outlines present certain diversities in the use of terms, but all have their individual advantages. A careful and thorough comparison of the terms used by different writers, therefore, cannot fail to throw a great deal of light upon the steps themselves. Most of the terms are, to some extent, self-explanatory; but they are by no means sufficient in themselves to give an adequate, thorough conception of their significance and application. It may be well, however, to emphasize that *Analysis* (as used by Herbart and Ziller) denotes merely analysis of the ideas already present in the child's mind, that are related to the new material. *Synthesis* is the apperception of the new through the old. Together they produce "Clearness of the Particulars." *System* is Classification, and *Method* is Function or Application.—*V. L.*

Supplementary Remarks upon the Formal Steps of Instruction.

This Herbartian principle is perhaps the most directly applicable of the three principles that refer especially to the material of instruction, because it deals with the independent class-work of the teacher, and does not necessarily conflict with any of the prescribed or traditional forms of the curriculum. Its psychological foundation, and general and theoretical phases have just been sufficiently presented. We shall now briefly consider the formal steps of instruction in their practical application. In so doing let us keep in mind the different terms by which they are known, since all possess a certain merit and are more or less suggestive. As a rule, however, we shall do well to use the terms Preparation, Presentation, Association, Generalization (including Classification), and Application, keeping constantly in mind that the first two are steps of the first chief stage, *Apperception*, the next two, steps in the second chief stage, *Abstraction*.

The approximate material for each year's work has been fixed upon in the curriculum. In this respect the teacher is necessarily somewhat limited. Within these limits, however, he should be granted abundant freedom; his first task, accordingly, is to divide the subject-matter for the year into a series of suitable method-wholes as set forth on page 140-41. The criterion of a well-chosen methodical unit is the single, chief, general truth which is embodied in its content. Its treatment requires a regular process of generalization. It is not so many pages of the text-book, nor so many problems, nor even a single chapter or subject as presented by the writer. All that the book contains aside from that which is necessary to complete each new, chief process of generalization, belongs to the fifth step, practice and application. Hence the task of fixing upon the methodical units is one that requires care and reflection. The sum of the method-wholes represents the total result that is to be attained within a given time. The compass of each method-whole, as regards time, cannot in general be determined. Let us, above all, beware of attempting to run through the five steps in each single hour or recitation. It is impossible to state, in general, whether the method-whole will occupy one, two, three, or more hours. This depends upon the branch of instruction and the development of the child. A method-whole in arithmetic, geometry, or physics, may often be completed in an hour, while one in geography, history, or language, may occupy several hours. The child will undoubtedly find less difficulty with the work in science, for example, after he has become accustomed to investigation.

The teacher's next task is to present the material contained in the method-whole to the pupil. The question arises at once, what is the most suitable way in which to introduce the work? The Herbartian practice generally places the "statement of the aim" at the head of the work upon each method-whole, a usage that is in direct opposition to the old practice of plunging straight into the subject-matter. But very often the method-wholes comprise the work of several days' recitation or several hours. In this case, after the statement of the main aim for the entire method-whole, it is necessary to present in succeeding hours, subordinate or partial aims, or hour-aims. The psychological considerations that demand the statement of the aim have been sufficiently stated on page 141. The statement of the aim of the lesson may be (1) a sentence which simply sets forth what the work of the new method-whole or of the ensuing hour will cover; (2) a question to which the teacher expects no answer, but which serves at once to give a certain tendency to the pupil's thoughts; (3) a problem or example which introduces some new mathematical or scientific method-whole containing a general truth at which the child is to arrive by the processes of apperception and abstraction.

The statement of the aim of the lesson is one of the pedagogical tasks in which the teacher should show the greatest skill, tact, originality, and freedom from fixed mechanical forms. Often the interest and success of an entire recitation depend upon the apt statement of the aim of the lesson. Accordingly, certain general rules must be observed. The statement of the aim must be simple and easily comprehensible. It should contain no unknown expressions or words, much less unknown conceptions. The statement of the aim must have a concrete content, and should never be merely formal; this is the point in which the teacher is most likely to err. For example, "We shall continue reading to-day where we left off yesterday," is absolutely fruitless and purposeless. Better, "To-day we shall see what became of Robinson after he was cast upon the island." The latter brings the child's thoughts at once to the required focus. Thoughts foreign to the work in hand are suppressed, and only related ideas busy the child's mind. This is the effect of the concrete content in the aim. The aim should be neither too scantily nor too broadly stated. In the first case the children still remain indifferent; in the second case the grasping of the chief point is rendered more difficult, and there is great danger that the pupils will anticipate too much. The statement of the lesson-aim should place the pupil in a state of expectation. If it is the chief aim of a complete method-whole it should be so formulated that a preliminary discussion of the method-whole may naturally follow. In this case also it should bring the connection with the historical series either directly or indirectly to the child's consciousness, as demanded by the principle of concentration. As a rule the chief aim of a method-whole should be given first by the teacher, while the subordinate aims will generally come spontaneously from the children and require but little correction. This privilege, at least, should never be denied them. The statement of the aim should be at the beginning of the hour or recitation, never after the recitation has begun. A new aim should not be introduced in the middle of the hour; that stated at the commencement of the recitation should comprehend the entire work of the lesson. Repetition of the aim is generally necessary, at least once. But the teacher should avoid unnecessary repetitions. A glance at the class will tell him when the aim has taken effect and its object been attained. If the aim introduces a method-whole it is followed at once by the first step.

Preparation.—Preparation proceeds at once from some conception contained in the aim. It analyzes the mental content of the child for the purpose of getting at the possible ideas upon the subject in hand that are already present in the child's mind. The purpose of preparation, therefore, is subservient to that of apperception; it aims to prepare the way for the acquisition of the new by calling up and ordering the related old. Hence preparation is analytic, while the following step, presentation, is synthetic. The two steps are to be clearly separated, however, for if they are *constantly com-*mingled during the instruction, the process of thought is checked and disturbed, the process of apperception does not achieve the desirable degree of clearness. This separation of preparation from presentation, however, does not exclude the possibility of dividing each into corresponding subdivisions, where the preparation would otherwise be too extended, an arrangement that is exceedingly necessary and advantageous when the method-whole deals with long narratives or descriptions. Accordingly in such cases as a method-whole in history, literature, geography, etc., well-defined portions of preparation may precede a corresponding portion of presentation. Another exception to the complete separation of preparation from presentation may be the "developing presentation" described on page 153.

Directly upon the statement and repetition of the aim, therefore, the teacher calls upon his pupils to relate what they already know of the subject. Sometimes a question or two will be necessary to set them to reflecting more deeply. It is far better, at first, to let the pupil be as independent as possible in the matter. If he is disposed to tell all he knows about the matter at once, he should not be interfered with, even though the order of his narrative is bad. If his instruction is properly directed from the moment he enters school, he will gradually acquire any orderly habit in speaking. But in the preparation let him be free. In behalf of unity in the circle of thought, the teacher should always aim to work with connected *series* of ideas, rather than with disconnected, *single* ideas. For this reason the stickler for questioning is a dangerous being to the child's power of independent, connected thought and expression. After one pupil has fully expressed himself, others may add whatever they can to the general stock. A few questions on the part of the teacher serve to cast out whatever the different pupils may have mentioned that is foreign to the subject, and to call out a more definite expression on the points that were insufficiently reproduced. The preparation may then be concluded by the orderly repetition of all that has been accepted. Here the teacher will do well to require the child to observe order and good expression as strictly as is consistent with the development of the child.

The preparation is generally longer in such branches as history, geography, reading, and shorter in such branches as geometry, arithmetic, botany, etc. It should cover so far as possible the entire content of the method-whole; but new material should not be drawn in with the old before the step of presentation; otherwise the expectation and interest are weakened. This demand, however, should not suppress the child's inclination freely to anticipate, and to construct in his own mind a picture of what is to follow. This picture may or may not harmonize with the reality, but both agreement and contrast are favourable to the process of acquisition. In order that the circle of thought may be thoroughly analyzed with reference to the new material about to be presented, exhaustive and extended considerations should be permitted. Non-essentials do not disturb the preparation, and can be finally eliminated. The child's ability at "rough-sketching" should be brought into action in the reproduction of his mental possessions wherever practicable.

Presentation.—After the orderly repetition of the material brought to light in the preparation, the instruction proceeds to the work of presenting the new. The material to be presented in a single method-whole cannot be assimilated by the child in a mass. The law of successive clearness[1] re-

---

[1] See De Garmo, *Essentials of Method*, p. 40.

quires that it be presented and assimilated in well-defined portions. Hence the material contained in each method-whole must be subdivided by certain suitable points of rest, each portion constituting in itself a unit. The points of rest give opportunity for absorption and reflection.[1] Each portion is to be treated separately and followed immediately by a connected reproduction. Only after the latter has taken place should a familiar discussion of the material take place. Here the teacher takes the opportunity to correct false impressions, throw light upon the dark points that appear during reproduction, and call for a statement of omissions from others. Each distinct portion of material may then be summed up under some appropriate heading, which at the close of the hour may be entered in a blank book kept for the purpose. The completion of all the several parts of a method-whole calls for a brief total reproduction.

The method of presentation is, of course, different for different branches. If the material appears in the form of a narrative, the latter should be free, objective, spirited, and adapted to the child's feeling. If the subject under consideration belongs to the strictly historical series, the total presentation and reproduction should be followed by a discussion directed by the teacher's questions for the purpose of drawing out the child's judgment upon the valuable ethical or esthetic relations contained in the method-whole. The child is led to a deeper insight into the true meaning and nature of events, an insight that must, of course, correspond to his own stage of development. If the aim of education in general, and of the historical series in particular, is not to be forgotten, this training of the child's ethical judgment through the historical should never be neglected nor superficially attempted. It is a task that requires the utmost care on the part of the teacher. This process of absorption, this deepening of the insight, should

---

[1] Vertiefung and Besinnung (Herbart).

never be introduced before the entire material of the historical method-whole has been presented. An ethical judgment can only be impartially developed when all the facts are known; otherwise the child's natural tendency to hasty judgment is fostered. The teacher should never allow the process of reflection and absorption to lapse into mere, dry, superficial moralizing.

In geography and the natural sciences presentation consists chiefly in observation and investigation of the subject of instruction, followed by a reproduction of the results of investigation. The child should be gradually accustomed to observe a fitting order in making his observations and to reproduce their results connectedly. Here, too, the *headings* are of great importance and must be chosen with a view to ater condensation and classification. In mathematics, presentation consists in the development of the solution of a typical concrete problem and the repetition of the solution. The initial problem must then be followed by others of the same nature, in order that a natural process of generalization may follow.

In general, two forms of presentation may be distinguished, (1) the narrative presentation and (2) the developing presentation.[1] The latter requires the greater skill on the part of the teacher. The former is most useful in historical instruction, where the material is either related by the teacher or read from the book. But it is a poor form for universal application. It cannot sufficiently call out the self-activity of the pupil, especially in such branches as the natural sciences, language, and mathematics. The developing presentation is applicable in all branches, and when skilfully handled gives the most satisfactory results. It is the only form in which the presentation may be blended, as

---

[1] "Erzählend darstellend" and "entwickelnd darstellend." The latter is now generally known as merely "darstellend."

it were, with the first step, preparation. It leads the child to construct the desired results from his own experiences and from that which his observations and reflection present to him. Here the teacher is the guide of the pupil in his endeavours at self-instruction. One danger, however, must be carefully avoided; the developing presentation should never lapse into a mere chain of leading questions. He applies the developing form of presentation best, who questions the least. An occasional question is unavoidable, and, indeed, desirable. A single remark or word on the part of the teacher should suffice to put the pupil on the right track when he has gone astray.

Reproduction should be free and originally expressed on the part of the pupil. The teacher should avoid interrupting the child's flow of thought except in cases of urgent necessity. The number of reproductions should be sufficient to insure that the material has been well impressed. Presentation, the same as preparation, should make constant use of rough sketching. The course of presentation is essentially the same whether a book is used or not. If the presentation is made through the book, the work may be studied after having been first before the class as a whole. In either case, where the presentation occupies several hours, each hour should be opened after the statement of the aim with the repetition of the previous day's work.

Association.—The third step (the first of abstraction) begins with the repetition of the synthetic material and its comparison and association with the old. This association, however, should not take place idly and without a plan. Only valuable associations, such as subserve the aim of the method-whole, are permissible. Especial value is to be attached to associations by means of which the child is finally brought to abstract the general truths contained in the concrete material of the method-whole. All observed cases are compared and their like elements noted. The new historical event is compared with the old and the similarity clearly expressed. One form, country, process, character, or event is compared with another.

The compared objects must always be known; especially fruitful is the comparison with objects from the child's own environment, intercourse, or experience. As can be readily seen, the third step, association, is followed closely and immediately by

Generalization (Classification).—The two steps, in fact, belong to one process, abstraction. Generalization first provides for the clear formation of the notional, of the concept. It brings the process of abstraction to completion. This requires (1) the separation of the notional from the concrete; (2) the formulation of the statement of the notional in language; (3) the placing of the concept thus attained in its proper place in already formed series of concepts (system), *i.e.* its classification; (4) the repetition and fastening of the concept. The latter includes the writing of the concept in the form of rules, maxims, etc., in a so-called system-book, with illustrations as examples where necessary. Where several subordinate associations or generalizations are to be drawn from the method-whole beside the main truth, as may frequently occur, each association should be followed directly by the corresponding generalization without the intervention of other associations.

The law, truth, or rule, *i.e.* the notional, is to be brought out by skilful questions, and sharply and completely separated from the concrete material, so that it is independent of all individual ideas or concepts. The notional is, in fact, not *separated* from the concrete so much as *distinguished* from it, for it is still dependent upon and connected with the latter. In the historical series the notional generally finds expression in an esthetical, ethical, social, or political maxim; in mathematics and language it culminates in a rule, and in science in the establishment of genera, families, etc., in classification, and in formulas. In both science and geography the fourth step presents in a brief and concise form the essential generalized results of the observations. The drawing of an *exact* map presents the best geographical system. We see therefore that in establishing the system of classification, the fourth step must constantly refer to past method-wholes; in fact, classification is frequently possible only after several method-wholes have been completed. When the general truth, maxim, or formula has once been obtained the next step is

Application.—This step has a twofold end in view: (1) the knowledge must obtain a certain degree of stability and mobility so that the mind shall be capable of commanding its services at will; (2) it must be diligently exercised upon practical questions, so that the child associates its use with the needs of life. There are various exercises of this kind. The series of ideas or concepts may be repeated forward and backward, from different starting-points and under different circumstances. The child may be required to descend from the concept to the individual perceptions (deduction) and *vice versâ* (induction). In the case of the historical instruction examples may be gathered from history or the child's life which either conform or do not conform to a given maxim. In the various branches of language-instruction, examples may be sought that conform to some grammatical rule, and conversely the pupil may determine which rule governs a given form, etc. Written and spoken exercises conform to the grammatical system which he has thus far attained. In mathematics and the natural sciences, the geometric, arithmetical, and physical formulas and laws may be applied in solving practical problems and tasks, or a physical apparatus may be drawn to conform to certain given conditions. In geography a general map may be sketched from memory, or commercial, physical and political facts applied in imaginary cases.

Because of their formal nature the formal steps of instruction have a universal application. Herbart himself said: "These rules are universal, and must be followed in all instruction without exception." But let us not begin to be fearful that our freedom and individuality in instruction are to be infringed by conforming to steps that bear the often dreaded term, "formal," and that claim a universal validity. They are simply guides that show how instruction must conform to the mental processes of the child in acquiring knowledge. The knowledge is not acquired until these steps have been taken, either consciously or unconsciously, skilfully or unskilfully, on the part of the teacher. The successful teacher, therefore, will find that the formal steps accord with much of his past practice, and that a clear and systematic knowledge of their requirements will render his future labours more fruitful. But let us emphasize once more that, within the inevitable psychical laws, the formal steps of instruction guarantee the teacher a far-sighted individuality and a rational freedom, such as slavish conformity to any other more specific method can never furnish. He is at liberty to determine their application to suit the needs of each single branch and to harmonize with the age and capacity of his pupils. Within each single step he is free to apply a great variety of devices and subordinated methods, to give free play to his ingenuity, and hence to relieve the monotony of instruction whenever it appears.

In closing, let us call attention to the fact that the formal steps stand in the closest relation to the historical stages and concentration. The three principles constitute a complete whole. The psychological bond that unites them may be found in the requirements of apperception. But even in the absence of the first two principles, either partly or entirely, the formal steps of instruction will be found applicable.[1]—*V. L.*]

---

[1] Compare C. A. McMurry's *General Method*, chapters v., vi., viii.

II. Special Didactics.

It is the task of special didactics to point out how the underlying principles of general didactics affect the organization of each single branch. Special didactics is entirely dependent on general didactics. This dependency must be carried out; it must be everywhere apparent; it must be evident even in the smallest part. Only under this condition can we claim to possess a system—a well-arranged organism. Only then do we arrive at a scientifically established theory of instruction, leave the standpoint of subjective caprice, and approach a knowledge of objective truth. Without the firm substructure, such as is vouched for by the results of general didactics, special didactics becomes exceedingly volatile, and scatters in as many fragments as there are subjects and ways of instruction.

If, as some think and claim, every branch of instruction is to develop its own course, its own methods, we shall finally be confronted by a motley miscellany which would present manifold ways in which man seeks to press on to the knowledge of things, it is true, but which sets the nature, growth, and development of the youthful mind aside. But one should not conceive that the characteristic features of the branches of knowledge are to be extinguished, suppressed, or crowded out by subjecting the principles of special didactics to those of general didactics. By no means,—this attempt would be just as useless as foolish. The ways of professional science and school science are very different. Here also the deeply-rooted distinction between the special sciences in their professional aspect and the sciences in the schools becomes glaringly apparent. Above all, a sharp distinction must be made; the ways which scientific research pursues in the different spheres, the methods by means of which the man of learning seeks to invade the kingdom of the unknown and the unexplored, cannot be the same in all respects as those which must guide the *youthful* mind that it may obtain an education. Therefore, he who aims to determine the course of procedure for each branch in the school by proceeding in accordance with the method of scientific research, will always find himself in the closest touch and most intimate accord with the results of science, it is true, but will always conflict with the psychological conditions under which the youthful mind is accustomed to perform its functions. If one has science *alone* in view, he argues the acquisition of knowledge merely from the standpoint of the scientific subject, without regard to psychical processes in the individual. And yet one must proceed from the latter if he wishes to *educate*, from the former only if he merely wishes to penetrate into the knowledge of things and disseminate science.

Therefore, the *fundamental method to be applied* does not indicate the nature of the science but the nature of the mind. General didactics teaches the general conditions under which the educator can so regulate the instruction of the youth that it shall be educative. It presents the principles to which the course of each separate branch must conform, but without neglecting the peculiar nature of the latter, even in the least. The principles remain, under all circumstances, the same. If they are true, they are, as fundamental laws of the human mind, eternal and unchangeable, the same as fundamental laws of Nature in general. But in the application to different materials their conformation changes, although their nature remains the same. Therefore, it is only correct to submit the methodical treatment of each subject of instruction to the respective special science when the latter at the same time accepts the underlying pedagogical principles as its universal guiding standards.

The latter, it is true, are not recognized by all as conclusive, either because the historical-philosophical foundations are doubted, or the psychological suppositions in their metaphysical and empirical phases censured, or because some will not allow themselves to have anything to do with pedagogy in general, and expect from it only an enfeeblement, an obscuration of the specific character of science, which must, above all, be retained. But we also recognize the latter claim in full. Scientific truth should never be sacrificed to some pre-conceived, theoretical, pedagogical arrangement, but the science in its professional character should never stand in the foreground; it must be subject to the authority of the general laws that lie at the foundation of didactics. Even with this restriction there is still scope enough to quiet all fears that violence may be done to the individual sciences between the wheels of the pedagogical mill.

Special didactics, also, should never indulge in the illusion that it is able alone to provide for the organic construction of the separate branches of study; it must always be referred to the assistance of the exact science, although, of course, it must not leave its task to the latter alone. The danger of an endless sundering, or of an entirely one-sided prosecution of studies lies but too near; didactics which gathers the scattered, unites the separate, and harmonizes the antithetical elements, must always be heard. Pedagogical didactics appears in the midst of the present great and constantly increasing differentiation and specialization of the sciences as a gatherer; with calm reflection, and free from all scientific factions, it extracts, accepts and applies those assured results of science that are necessary for the education of the youth, and always keeps the whole in view, in spite of all details that draw the attention into byways. From this standpoint the task of special didactics appears in truth as a great and difficult one. The different rays from the various departments of knowledge focus here; comprehended under common points of view, they present a whole, a system, an order which does not desire to point out new roads for exact science (although this is by no means excluded), so much as to place the pupil in possession of a reliable mental content, and the proper method of its acquisition.

One should never forget that pedagogics and didactics are *scientific* subjects, and not mere facilities, as it were, that could be drilled in; they are scientific subjects in so far as they rest upon fundamental conceptions. These underlying ideas are fundamental, for they are based upon ethical, historical-philosophical, and psychological reflections. The methodical treatment of the separate branches, accordingly, can only be submitted to the care of the special sciences when the latter, armed with an exact knowledge of the subject, adapt their didactic treatment to the fundamental ideas, and thus become the necessary complement of general and special didactics. The latter, which are concerned with a large number of subjects, can never enter into the details as thoroughly as each branch of science does for itself. Under the above-mentioned condition we bid the co-operation of the special sciences welcome. On the other hand, whenever they attempt to free themselves from the general foundation for the purpose of building independently, we regard the work as fatal, because it creates a chaos of disconnected precepts that mutually check, if they do not entirely remove, one another's effects.

Just as the proposition: "Every teacher must have his own method," is valid only in a certain sense as regards the personality of the teacher, so the proposition: "Each branch of instruction has its own method," has only a very limited validity. In either case one is far from true science, which refers both the personality of the teacher and the individual sciences as soon as they enter into the service of education, to the psychical laws that lie at the foundation of the development of the youthful mind. No natural education whatever is conceivable without a careful consideration of these laws.

THE THEORY OF GUIDANCE.

We generally distinguish two departments in the subject of guidance: (1) The theory of *training* (moral training) and (2) the theory of *government*. Government comprehends more the outer, training more the inner measures for guidance; the former is directed to the present, the latter looks to the future; the former will above all else effect external order, such as every well-regulated community, and hence also the school community, requires; the latter aims to produce some effect upon the disposition, and to provide for the formation of character. This influence is the essential factor, in comparison with which all those measures that are not directly connected with the formation of the disposition and character seem to be of less importance. These latter are comprehended under the term, "government," the former under the term, "training." In practice the measures adopted by both often coincide; in this case the boundary between them is unnoticeable. Theoretically, however, it is of value to the educator to be able to review his measures suitably, to judge of their range, and to be prepared to make the finest distinctions.

I. Theory of Training.

If the instruction is managed in the manner above described, its influence upon the education of the will and hence upon the formation of the character may become very effective. But even if the instruction has met all the requirements placed upon it, the school has not yet by any means discharged its appointed task. The work of instruction is, in fact, prominent, but it is not the only task.

It is assisted by *guidance*, the educative activity in the narrower sense, which constitutes an effective aid in attaining the proposed end. The indirect formation of character should find an efficient support in the direct. "Educate so that the pupil will guide himself, choosing the good and rejecting the evil;" this, according to Herbart, is the formation of moral character. The elevation to a self-conscious personality should without doubt be effected in the disposition of the pupil through his own activity; it would be folly for the educator to attempt to create the very essence of the power that underlies this self-conscious elevation. But he must hold it possible to place the power which is already at hand, and which is necessarily true to its own nature, in such a condition that it can be relied upon to accomplish the moral elevation of the individual. The educator must regard it as the chief office of his endeavours to bring about, establish, and further the permanent activity of this power.

We proceed from the thought that the activity of the will is to receive a definite tendency toward the good. The educator should provide that all future activity of the will bears the stamp of a personality that has placed its volition exclusively in the service of the moral ideas. The ultimate aim of education is directed to the formation of an ethical character. Character is not an original fruit of the intellectual life; neither is it one that ripens easily or under all circumstances. Otherwise, why should this fruit be so rare?

The educator must investigate exactly the conditions under which a character, especially a moral character develops. Here psychology is an important aid to him. The central point of moral development is the formation of maxims, of practical principles. We determine the degree of one's culture by that which he considers as bidden or forbidden, by his maxims. That man stands upon the lowest stage of culture whose maxims are only maxims of sensual gratification, who seeks merely the sensually pleasurable, avoids merely the sensually disagreeable. We regard the maxims of wisdom, of the useful, of the becoming, of the fitting and unfitting as standing upon a higher plane. The moral maxims that have to do with the will itself without regard to foreign motives, and the sum of whose contents we call conscience or practical insight, stand upon the highest plane.

Now the different maxims may agree with or contradict one another. If the latter is the case, that maxim will be followed which has the greatest power in the mind. A contest, a reflective comparison of the worth of the various principles, precedes the decision. Thus by degrees an order or system of the maxims is produced. The consistency and uniformity of the will, which constitute the essence of character, rest upon the subjection of the entire volitional activity to this system. A character whose supreme principles are the moral ideas, and which, therefore, subjects its entire volition to the voice of conscience, is a moral character. We distinguish two phases: (1)

single acts of the will, or a manifold volition produced by the desires; (2) a general volition, *i.e.* a volition that is self-developing in the mass of apperceived ideas. The former is that which is determinable, the latter is that which determines; the former is the *objective*, the latter the *subjective* phase of the character. This distinction is important for training.

The first presupposition is that efficiency and vigour of the will, of the inner activity, be present. The *instruction* seeks to secure this efficiency by the presentation of numerous "pictures of the will" in ideal intercourse, history, literature, etc. But can the task of *training* be based upon this work? Here it would seem as if human power were powerless to do or make, and must be content to look on. But this is not the case. It is true that education itself can make no alterations so far as inherited physical and intellectual disposition is concerned, but it will still be able to prevent evil influences, just as the educator is able to accomplish a great deal that at first appeared impossible as regards the pupil's position and manner of life. Many wishes and inclinations to whose gratification the mode of life has accustomed the child, many aspirations and sentiments which have their foundation in the conditions under which he grows up or in the distinctive views of his class, appear ineradicable; and yet, through the determinative influence of the educator a great deal can be checked and removed. Desire and love for a great many things can be generated. In fact, instruction will also be helpful here by means of that which it teaches the child; but although it succeeds in convincing the pupil of the untenableness of its prejudices and aspirations, the newly acquired ideas will still often be insufficiently powerful to suppress certain evils to which the scholar has been accustomed from childhood. In this case the measures necessary for training must come to the aid of instruction. Of course, both instruction and training are sometimes compelled to give up trying to counteract successfully the more powerful conditions and obstructions over which they have no control; these gave the pupil's will a tendency which runs counter to the purpose of education before instruction and training began, and their influence never ceases. The educator has no power whatever over these forces that are in part invisible; he cannot control the occult coadjutors of education. If they are mightier than the systematic measures of the educator, he can only hope that unforeseen events and changes will enter the inner and outer life of the child and overpower everything in the disposition which opposes his efforts. Many a one has been converted only by the harsh blows of fortune, by an unsuspected radical change of his condition in life, by an intimate friendship, by absorption in religious thoughts and feelings, by great convulsing events. It is the business of the educator to avail himself of such occurrences in the life of the pupil as long as he stands at his side, and to provide that the convulsion of the child's inner life lead to a transformation in accordance with the purpose of education, and that the influence of the experience be made as deep and lasting as possible.

We shall now consider the measures to be undertaken by training in this direction somewhat more closely.

As we have said before, the objective side of the character appears first; accordingly the care of the educator must be directed to the cultivation of an efficient objective will. Hence it is necessary to give opportunity for various actions that correspond to the moral law. We are not speaking in favour of a vast deal of activity, but of a systematic regular activity, be it at first only in play. The regimen of the family with its occupations, commissions, mutual services, etc., offer an especially favourable opportunity; but there is also no lack of opportunities for various activities, and hence for training the will in the school life. Here we have in mind the school works and all the activities which a well-arranged school life brings with it. These various activities, although often apparently insignificant, are instituted for the sake of their educative value, and clothed with some official dignity in order to make them more effective. We have also in mind the works in the school garden and the school workshop. Here every successful act constitutes a source of future volition and action; for the successful deed is at the same time a school for the courage. Although the way appears shorter, the task easier to a child of courage, the educator still knows that evil spirits have freer play in the spiritless, faint-hearted, cowardly dispositions, and on this account regards courage as a welcome companion in his work.

Just as the educational effect of the home is greater in proportion to the constancy of its regimen, so also the school not only has the means of developing the virtues of love of order, punctuality, and diligence, by the constancy of its order and the regularity of its life, but also becomes thereby a school of the will. That which the school is able to accomplish as regards the development of fixed habits, however, appears small in comparison with the influence of the home. On the other hand, it controls another means that is of special importance for our purpose, *viz.* the school community. Although in the family common joy and common woe, common work and common recreation exercise a great influence upon the formation of the child's view of life and the tendency of the will, an influence which, be it injurious or beneficial, continues to be effective throughout the entire life,—the *narrow limitations* of the family life often contrast so sharply with the gaiety and diversity in the world that a direct transition from the one to the other implies great dangers. Here the school offers itself as mediator between these two extremes, as an institution that presents in a form adapted to the youth a sort of imitation of the future social life. The larger circle of companions of the same age, whom the pupil finds in the school, will make the latter a fit institution to effect the transition from the family to the world. Furthermore, if the *full* strength of character can only be acquired in the stream of life, the initial steps toward its acquirement are most suitably taken in a circle which stands mid-way between the family and the great circle of human society. This is the school community in which there is no lack of the frictions so necessary for the formation of character. Here, especially, one finds that active intercourse upon the playground, in the gymnasium, during rambles and excursions, on holidays and at celebrations, which calls out the child's own activity, a result so important for the training of the will. Many errors will be more easily removed here than in the family. When on these occasions the arrogant and stubborn youth is left unnoticed, the vain and visionary one shamed, the proud humbled, the thoughtlessly awkward derided, the lazy hustled along, the timid encouraged, and the delicate hardened, the effect of such educational measures is so much the more forcible because their application was spontaneous. It is true that real errors may also develop in this social life (as, for example, the mischievous nature that finds pleasure in rendering others uncomfortable or ridiculous, or the one that is ambitious to place himself in the foreground), but this is no ground against emphasizing the importance of just this educational factor, for various means of eradicating such errors are at the command of the judicious teacher. Let us now consider, furthermore, that the life of the school community compels the individual to subordinate himself to the interests of the whole, that the lively feeling of fellowship does not permit the errors of intolerance, dogmatism, lust of power and selfishness to prevail. By fostering this feeling, the child is also prepared for the intercourse of after-life, in which the individual only finds his proper place when he feels that he is a member of various larger and smaller social communities, in which he only fulfils his task in life by participating in the interests and endeavours of his contemporaries according to the measure of his power, not by retiring in selfish narrow-mindedness. The school educates for civil life, in that it educates for the school life; its effect is that of a united whole, which it is. The individual should attach himself to this whole; he must subordinate himself to the entire body and take his proper place as one of its members. The school is to the scholar a state, a small corporate body, which he can understand and survey at a glance, in whose service he learns how one should serve the whole and feel himself in harmony with the whole, how the entire body stands higher and is of much more worth and importance than the individual with his pretentious claims, than the ego with its selfishness. Therefore, in the school there are no exclusive privileges, no exceptions, no partial preferences!

The ideal to which the school must aspire, is the fusion of the school community to a *united ethical personality*, whose head is the educator or the community of educators. All those impulses will also be felt here that constantly incite the individual as a member of an ethical community; above all, the sympathetic feelings, which constitute the foundation of genuine benevolence, and a common spirit, which will be of a moral nature if the community stands in the right relations to the educator. The better elements will then obtain the control and hold the bad elements in check. Of course, if the educator has not understood how to bring about the proper confidential relations between himself and his pupils, the state of affairs is reversed in that he is regarded as the natural enemy of youth. In this way a great many errors arise which threaten to reverse the educational effect. Here it becomes evident *how important a part the personality of the educator plays*. One may say, in fact, that the entire educational centre of gravity lies in the personality of the teacher. If he is candid and true, conscientious and competent, consistent and just, if he has command of himself in all situations and in all cases, if he is neither malicious nor inclined to anger, in short, if he is a complete man, the dark forces cannot thrive in the community of the school. Thus it becomes clearly evident that it would be a foolish undertaking to attempt an ethical education merely with the aid of instruction. The character of the teacher, his example in judging and acting, his conduct both in doing and permitting, are of such great significance that even the most carefully devised method is unable to remove or balance the errors and defects in the personality of the educator. Uninterruptedly and unintentionally, as Ziller has shown, the example of the educator exerts either an elevating or a depressive influence upon the inner life of each individual pupil. The silent force of his influence is almost as important as the force of those relations under whose combined effect ethical personality develops; hence, it surely is not surpassed by the formative influence of the instruction, in so far as the will and the disposition of the pupil are concerned. This appreciation of the force of personality, however, should produce neither an under-valuation of methodical practice, nor a contempt for all pedagogical reflections; on the contrary, the two factors are of equal value. No natural educator is so gifted through divine favour from the beginning, as to be able to reach the highest results entirely without the aid of all methodical schooling, and there will never be a method so wonderful as to be able to supplant the power of strong personality. Therefore, the educator who undertakes his office in earnest will constantly direct his attention to the perfection of the *method* of instruction, and at the same time labour to develop and perfect his own personality, because so many factors that are important for the success of direct education, depend upon his conduct, his example and his appearance. There are still other devices at the command of the educator for awakening, fostering, and preserving a healthy spirit and life in the community of the school and which furnish an especially advantageous approach to the hearts of the children. These are the *school celebrations* and *holidays*, the *school-walks* and *school-journeys*. Their value is exceedingly great. In the first place, they offer many opportunities for the self-activity of the pupil; then they also give opportunity for the exchange of other thoughts than those with which the instruction is occupied. Common joys, recreations and exertions not only unite teacher and scholars, but also strengthen the fellowship of the school companions.

Still another form of school observance is of especial importance because it is of great value in the formation of the ethical will. Morality will necessarily remain a wretched plant of unnatural growth if its religious consecration is wanting, if it is not fostered and nourished by a trust in God. But as the religious interest finds not only its expression, but also its nourishment in the religious services of the community, so also regular *school devotions* that are in unison with the feelings and aspirations of the child's heart may be effective in furthering his religious and moral life.

Those means that have thus far been discussed and fixed upon as necessary measures of guidance in the formation of character, affect chiefly its objective side.

They extend only to the single acts of the will that are called forth by the educative influence, and whose effect upon the formation of character is greater the less these acts are isolated, the more their power is strengthened by habit. Now, if the *subjective* side of the character, a general volitional activity rooted in the prevailing circle of thought, develop spontaneously in accordance with the laws of the mental life from the single acts of the will, the education should not neglect this process of abstraction.

That which the objective phase of the character has gained by a systematic and intelligent guidance, by watchful and constructive care, is at first only the result of a foreign influence. When the pupil has been brought to regard his own moral culture as a serious and important affair, training and instruction in combination with the child's growing knowledge of the world, can cause a moral fervour to penetrate his entire circle of thought; they can, then, provide that the pupil's idea of the moral order of the world be constantly associated on the one hand with his religious ideas, on the other hand with his introspection. Then training may withdraw, and the further development of the character be safely left to the pupil's own work.

The following synopsis gives a brief review of the arrangements which training may institute and carry into effect to further the culture of an ethical will.

Arrangement of the School Life as Sustained by a Common Interest.

1. School devotions and religious services for children.

2. School celebrations of all kinds.

3. School-walks and school-journeys.

4. Offices or duties (various functions to be performed in the garden, workshop, schoolroom and school library).

5. The preparation of character sketches (Individualization).[1]

The perfection of the personality should, and must be the work of one's own insight and free choice, as has already been emphasized. As long as this is not the case there is no guarantee that other, newer, and perhaps more powerful influences than the former will not suddenly overthrow all that has been attained. This is to be prevented by the cultivation of the subjective side of the character; the moral maxims should attain such a mastery in the soul of the pupil that everything is measured by them But the firm establishment of the practical principles, of course, will only be reached in the period of independent action, a period that lies beyond the range of school education. The educator, therefore, can only exert a limited influence upon its formation. He can prepare the way and lay the foundation; but the acquisition of the subjective, moral character, as a fixed possession, is the result of every man's own labour. How could it be otherwise? Here we have to do with an internal process of development which advances but slowly and which never entirely terminates even in the noblest and best character.

The subjective phase of the adult character appears in the form of firm principles as opposed to the con-

---

[1] Which rests entirely in the hands of the teacher, of course.

fused host of desires and resolutions. But it requires a long process of development. The imperceptible beginnings are made in the first moments of the incipient self-observation. From this time on, precepts and rules appear, which correspond to the importance of the previous inclinations, habits, and activities; in proportion as the education progresses these precepts become universal maxims or general rules for all future cases. Thus, reflection brings the process of generalization and subsumption into activity by means of which the individual's own body of laws in the form of a system of principles develops naturally to a greater universality.

Is it not natural that training should always be vigilant and ready to accompany with council and deed the important formations that take place in the inner life of the pupil in accordance with natural laws? Is it not a common experience that maxims and the requirements of the moral laws are often well understood but gain no influence over the will? Does not the pupil easily go astray because the deed that has once succeeded but too easily becomes the source of another similar act of the will? He who has often so successfully gained his point in pursuing a certain advantage, who has often enjoyed the reputation of wisdom by following some seductive precedent, who, under favourable circumstances, has often found the right help through bad intercourse, can easily become a different person as to his inclinations and purposes than the educator desires. But very little is required to debase the inner, moral standard, so that the maxims of wisdom receive the first place, the moral disposition the second place. The guidance of the educator can overcome this danger by furnishing protection and support, by appealing to the conscience of the child and providing that the moral ideas gradually obtain command over him.

The chief condition for a proper guidance is a right relation between educator and pupil. The necessary corrections of the child's judgments, estimations and requests must always be regarded and received as a service of friendship, but not as an officious invasion. Otherwise the effect is entirely lost; reserve and retirement are the immediate consequence. Of course different natures are very differently endowed as regards their ability for self-observation and self-government; therefore, for the same reason the activity of the educator is also very different in each case. It is difficult to give the educator definite directions, simply because the number of individual cases is so great; because the same measure may produce a very different effect at different times.

By way of summary we may say with Herbart—(1) Training should restrain. Where the memory of the will is deficient, where thoughtlessness takes its place, it is necessary to give stability to the pupil. He must know that he cannot go beyond certain limits; he must have a lively feeling that he possesses something in the *satisfaction* of his teacher which he will not willingly lose. (2) Training should exert a determinative influence. It should cause the *pupil* to choose, not the educator. (3) Training should regulate, *i.e.* the educator should not leave the pupil entirely to himself as soon as he begins to reflect upon acts that are permitted and not permitted. Training must take measures to prevent a false determination. He who lightly establishes his precepts must be made to feel how difficult it is to act in accordance with them.

All this presupposes a constant, intimate intercourse between educator and pupil. The educator must understand how to bend his intellect to the world of the children; he must acquire sympathy for the inclinations, wishes, and moods of the little ones; he must think, feel and will with them; then he can succeed in guiding and educating them. But the guidance of the teacher has achieved a great deal when the pupil has reached the point at which he fears nothing more than to find himself, upon inner self-examination, despicable and reprehensible in his own eyes, when he endeavours to bring his will into accord with the moral law, so that he cannot help despising himself if he does not obey.

II. The Government of Children.

Government comprehends the system of measures by which the expressions and actions that do not issue from the hearts of the children are restrained and guided so as not to disturb the educative work of instruction and training. All the pure impulses of an unbridled natural power, of a wild impetuosity, must often be held in check by much stronger means than certain intense manifestations of the pupil's will, which are very important in themselves, but require a much more delicate handling. The measures that are taken for government, aim above all to create and preserve order. All incivilities, all disturbances, all disorders should be removed; in fact, if possible, they should not appear at all, but should be nipped in the bud. If the will of the child is not to receive an uncompanionable tendency, he should be made to feel early and constantly the restraint which every individual within a community must bear. Government, therefore, aims to attain no direct end whatever in the mind of the child, but will only produce order; it aims to be felt as a power that is concerned with nothing further than the enforcement of its measures. For this purpose various measures are at command which may be classed—(1) as those that prevent disorder, and (2) as those that suppress disorder. To the former belong, above all, the suitable occupation of the children. If they are well employed, if the proper change between work and recreation takes place, their thoughts are generally far from disturbance. Furthermore, a suitable supervision will be able to nip many disorders in the bud. For the removal of disorders that have already arisen, the reprimand, the threat and the punishment are at the disposal of the educator.

Experience shows that we cannot get along in education *without punishment.* A glance at the history of education teaches what an important part it played in former times, when it was almost regarded as the only means of education. With the progress of humanity there has been an increase of the efforts to use that means of education most sparingly which is the most powerful, but hence least free from danger.

This tendency is to be welcomed, because the sparing use of punishments increases their efficacy while their continual application, often without a clear motive, only serves to blunt the effect. The purpose of punishment lies entirely within in the educational system; it should help educate; it should combat the errors which the child commits. By breaking through the natural course of inner activity in some impressive way, it compels the mind of the child to reflect upon itself, and this is its purpose. It desires to produce introspection in the one who has been punished, to make him sufficiently attentive to that which is taking place within his inner life. Here he must find that the punishment was deserved. When this is the case the punishment is properly effective and leads to improvement, if the further activity of the educator supplements it by preventing two great temptations, and by supporting and encouraging higher interests. Since the efficacy of the punishment rests upon the disturbance of the emotional life that it produces, on that account it should never become a daily or common occurrence. Every mere repetition finds the emotional life duller; the pupil is already prepared for it, expects it; it can impart no significant impulse to his train of thoughts. Therefore every punishment must be adapted to the individual character of each pupil; time and attendant circumstances must also be taken into account. On the other hand we may say that the rareness with which the educator is compelled to have recourse to the severer forms of punishment, affords a safe standard by which to estimate his art. The better the education is, so much the more may the punishment be dispensed with. Therefore the first law to be established here may be stated as follows: One must educate so that he will need to use punishment as little as possible.

But even the most careful education cannot withhold all evil from the heart of the child. Especially the energetic natures cannot be educated to obey freely without punishments. Free obedience, which leads to moral independence, consists in the proper insight into that which is bidden, and the will to think and act in accordance with this insight. Accordingly, two kinds of punishments may be distinguished: (1) punishment which increases the *insight*, punishment as a *warning*; (2) punishment which influences the *will*, the *moral* punishment.

With these two forms of punishment is associated a third, namely, punishment which is applied merely for the purpose of discouraging certain acts. All aim to produce unconditional obedience in the pupil. But while government aims primarily only at submission on the part of the pupil, in that it does not attempt to act with the aid of underlying motives at all, training seeks to effect free obedience; it softens the harshness of the government in that it connects obedience closely with the child's own will.

Above all, education must proceed uniformly and consistently in matters of government. A quiet, firm decision, permeated by love and sustained by dignity, will win the hearts of the youth and guide them safely. All disparity in bidding and forbidding, hesitation in the matters of punishment and reprimand, will avenge themselves bitterly and prepare many troubled hours for the teacher.

As soon as possible government must be dispensed with, and training in connection with instruction must carry on the business of education alone.

III. Physical Education.

Among the external measures which the educator must apply, are those especially which are devoted to the physical education of the child. While the measures for government are gradually withdrawn as soon as fixed habits and fixed morals have been developed, the care for the bodily growth and vigour will never relax, but remain a true and vigilant co-worker in the development of the child.

The multifarious business activity of the present is placing increased burdens upon the body, especially upon the nervous system as the medium of the mental labour. On this account, the present race is especially admonished to retain this body in health and vigour, in order that the individual may be able to meet the greater demands of the present. The more we remove ourselves from the state of Nature, so much the more unfavourable do the conditions for the preservation of the physical health appear, so much the more do we lose the natural instinct for that which is of advantage to us physically. This fact argues the necessity for the care of the public health, which should extend also to the scholars. Here it appears in the form of school hygiene or the theory of health in school. It has nothing to do with the cure of diseases, but merely with the precautions that are to be taken against disease. How many individuals, later in life, carry on a silent but constant battle against the defective disposition and functional irregularity of their bodies, especially of their nervous systems. How often the battle is in vain, for the seeds of disease were sown in early youth, increased with years and spread as long as the individual was not especially admonished with regard to his health.

Since the health and power of the mind also depend upon the physical health, because of the intimate reciprocal action between body and mind, the importance of the bearer of the mental life shows the educator very forcibly that he should not neglect the care of the body, if he does not desire to render the success of his work in general questionable. For although he has firmly laid the foundations of moral character in the soul of his pupil and cherishes the hope that the latter can some day act and work as a complete man in the family, the community and the state, what does all this avail if it has been gained at the cost of bodily health? And what is true of the individual is true of the people. Of what advantage is it to a nation to achieve ever so lofty an intellectual culture, if the strength, health, and elasticity of the body does not keep pace with it? Must not that catastrophe then occur which history exemplifies in the Roman Empire of the world,—a highly cultivated people and a highly cultivated state, shattered by the Germanic tribes, who stood far behind in culture, but who could throw their youthful, fresh, physical power into the scales? Hence the State education must be intent upon preserving this physical energy with the aid of special devices. It will accomplish nothing, however, as long as the education of the single individual does not include the attentive care and thorough consideration of the bodily growth and vigour.

Thus a new and broad field of study and activity is open to the educator. A knowledge of the most necessary conditions of physical thrift is required of him; in this new sphere a new science offers its assistance, namely, *Physiology*, and especially *Hygiene*, whose teachings as regards means of nourishment, manner of living, clothing, etc., are of fundamental importance to the educator.

As already mentioned, a great deal has recently been accomplished in this line that is worthy of recognition. The number of writings that have already appeared upon the subject is very great. The impulse was given by the book of the physician Lorinser, 1886, *Zum Schutz der Gesundheit in den Schulen* ("On the Care of Health in the Schools"). Since then, the complaint that this side of education in the schools has been sadly neglected has never been silenced. Propositions have often been submitted for remedying the evil. The literature upon the subject treats (1) of the problem as a whole; (2) of care as regards the proper conditions of warmth, air, etc. (schoolhouse); (3) of care of the power of sight and physical growth (school desk).

The principles which education establishes for the care of the body must be reinforced by a system of gymnastic measures, free exercises, marching exercises with and without song or music, and games (football, base-ball, etc.), based upon anatomical and physiological principles and designed to render the body pliant, and as capable as possible of intercourse with the outer world.

THE END.

LITERARY REFERENCES.

The asterisk (*) denotes literature that belongs properly to the Herbartian School.

GENERAL PEDAGOGICS.

*Ackermann, Formale Bildung. *Langensalza.*
*Ackermann, Pädagogische Fragen. 2d series. *Dresden.*
Baur, Grundzüge der Erziehungslehre. 4th ed. *Giessen*, 1887.
Beneke, Erziehungs und Unterrichtslehre. 2 vols., 3d ed. *Berlin,* 1864.
Böhm, Praktische Erziehungslehre. 2d ed. *Munich*, 1890.
—— Praktische Unterrichtslehre. 2d ed. *Ib.*, 1890.
Dilthey, Ueber die Möglichkeit einer allgemeingültigen pädagog. Wissenschaft. *Berlin*, 1888.
*Frick-Meier, Sammlung pädag. Abhandlungen. *Halle.*
Gräfe, Allgem. Pädagogik. 2 vols. *Leipzig*, 1845.
Hegel's Ansichten über Erziehung und Unterricht. 3 T., hrsg. v. Thaulow. *Kiel*, 1835.
*Herbart, Pädagog. Schriften, hrsg. v. Willmann. 2 vols. *Leipzig.*
Jacoby, Allgemeine Pädagogik. *Gotha*, 1883.
Israel, Sammlung selten gewordener pädagog. Schriften. *Zschopau.*
Kehrbach, Monumenta Germaniæ pædagogica. *Berlin.*
—— Mitteilungen der Gesellschaft für deutsche Erziehungs-u. Schulgeschichte. Vol. i. *Berlin*, 1891.
*Kern, Grundriss der Pädagogik. 4th ed. *Berlin*, 1887.
*Lindner, Encyklopäd. Handbuch der Erziehungskunde. *Vienna* 1884.
—— Allgem. Erziehungslehre. 7th ed. *Ib.*, 1890.
—— Allgem. Unterrichtslehre. 7th ed. *Ib.*, 1890.
Niemeyer, Grundsätze der Erziehung und des Unterrichts. Ed. by Rein. *Langensalza.*
Palmer, Evangel. Pädagogik. 5th ed. *Stuttgart*, 1882.
*Rein, Pädagog. Studien; alte Folge. 2 vols. *Vienna.*
—— Neue Folge (since 1880). *Dresden.*
Richter, Neudrucke pädagog. Schriften. *Leipzig.*
——Jean Paul, Levana. Ed. by Lange. *Langensalza.*
——Levana for English readers. Ed. by Susan Wood, B.Sc. *London:* Swan Sonnenschein & Co. 1887.
Rosenkranz, Die Pädagogik als System. *Königsberg*, 1848. Translated by Anna C. Brackett. (The sub. tit. Philosophy of Education.) Vol. I. of the International Educ. Series. Ed. by Dr. W. T. Harris.
Sander, Lexikon der Pädagogik. 2d ed. *Breslau*, 1889.
*Schiller, Handbuch der prakt. Pädagogik. 2d ed. *Leipzig*, 1889.

Schleiermacher, Pädagog. Schriften, hrsg. v. Platz. *Langensalza.*
Schmid, Encyklopädie des ges. Erziehungs-und Unterrichtswesens. 2d ed. *Gotha.*
Schwarz-Curtmann, Lehrbuch der Erziehungs-und Unterrichtslehre. 7th ed. *Heidelberg*, 1866.
Schreber, Das Buch der Erziehung. *Leipzig.*
*Stoy, Encyklopädie der Pädagogik. 2d ed. *Leipzig*, 1878.
*Strümpell, Psychologische Pädagogik. *Leipzig*, 1880.
—— Pädagogische Pathologie. *Leipzig*, 1890.
*Waitz, Allgem. Pädagogik, hrsg. v. Willmann. 3d ed. *Brunswick.*
*Willmann, Didaktik. 2 vols. *Brunswick*, 1882-89.
*Ziller, Einleitung in die allg Pädagogik. *Leipzig*, 1856. Allg. Pädagogik. 3d ed., hrsg. v. Just. *Leipzig.*
*Ziller-Vogt, Jahrbücher des Verein fsür wiss. Pädagogik. 24 vols. *Dresden.*

Pedagogical Classics.

1. Beyer's Bibliothek. *Langensalza.*
2. Lindner, Pädagog. Klassiker. *Vienna.*
3. Richter's Bibliothek. *Leipzig.*

I. PRACTICAL PEDAGOGICS.

(A) THE FORMS OF EDUCATION.

1. HOME PEDAGOGICS.

*Ackermann, Die häusliche Erziehung. *Langensalza*, 1888.
Riehl, Die Familie. *Stuttgart.*
*Stoy, Hauspädagogik. *Leipzig*, 1855.
*Trüper, Die Familienrechte an der Erziehung. 2d ed. *Langensalza*, 1892.

2. SPECIAL EDUCATIONAL INSTITUTIONS.

Schmid, Encyklopädie : Alumnat und Erziehungsanstalt.

Education of the Deaf and Dumb.

Hill, Der gegenwärtige Zustand des Taubstummenunterrichts. *Essen*, 1886.
Matthias Vatter, Zeitschrist für Taubst.-u. Blindenanstalten ; since 1855. *Frankfurt.*
*Oehlwein, Meine Erfahrungen u. Ansichten über das Wesen der Vier-und Schwachsinnigen, etc. *Weimar*, 1883.
Schmid, Encyklopädie IX.
Walther, Geschichte des Taubstummenbildungswesens. *Leipzig*, 1883.
Walther u. Töpler, Blätter für Taubstummenbildung. *Berlin*, 1887.

Education of the Blind.

Fuchs, Die Ursachen und die Verhütung der Blindheit. *Wiesbaden,* 1885.
Knie, Anleitung zur zweckmässigen Behandlung blinder Kinder. 4th ed. *Berlin,* 1851.
Mecker, Der Blindenfreund ; since 1880. *Düren.*
Merle, Söder, Sengelmann, Das Blinden - Idioten - u. Taubstummenbildungswesen. *Norden,* 1887.
Pablasek, Die Blindenanstalten. *Vienna,* 1876.
Ruppert, Ueber Erziehung, Unterricht u. Versorgung d. Blinden. *Munich,* 1877.

Education of Idiots.

Brandes, Der Idiotismus und die Idiotenanstalten. *Hanover,* 1862.
Emminghaus, Die psychischen Störungen im Kindesalter. *Tübingen,* 1887.
Foerster, Der geistig Zurückgebliebene u. seine Pflege. *Dresden-Blasewitz,* 1888.
Griesinger, Pathologie und Therapie der psychischen Krankheiten. 4th ed. *Brunswick,* 1876.
Knapp, Beobachtungen über Idioten-und Kretinen-Anstalten und deren Resultate. *Graz,* 1879.
—— Besuch von Idiotenanstalten, etc. *Graz,* 1881.
Laehr, Die Idiotenanstalten Deutschlands. *Berlin,* 1874.
Zeitschrift für Idiotenwesen. *Dresden;* since 1881.

Reformatories.

Busch, Monatsschrift für innere Mission. *Gütersloh,* 1880.
Hübner, Heilpädagog. Zeitschrift. *Vienna,* 1871.
Jung, Knabenhort. *Munich,* 1885.
Oetker, Ueber Erziehungsanstalten für verwahrloste Kinder. *Berlin,* 1879.
Ranke. Gründung, Unterhaltung u. Leitung von Krippen, Bewahranstalten, etc. 7th ed. *Elberfeld,* 1886.
Wichern-Henske, Schmid's Encyklopädie VII. 2d ed. 1886.

3. School Education.

(a) The People's Schools.

Bock, Wegweiser. 4th ed. *Breslau,* 1869.
Denzel, Einleitung in die Erziehungs-und Unterrichtslehre. 3 parts. *Stuttgart,* 1825-35.
Diesterweg, Wegweiser. 5th ed. *Essen.*
*Dörpfeld, Zwei pädagogische Gutachten. *Gütersloh,* 1877.
Gräfe, Die deutsche Volksschule. 3d ed. *Leipzig.*
Harnisch, Handbuch für das deutsche Volksschulwesen. 3d ed. *Breslau,* 1839.
Heppe, Geschichte des deutschen Volksschulwesens. 5 vols. *Gotha,* 1858-60.
Kahle, Grundzüge der evang. Volksschulerziehung. 5th ed. *Breslau,* 1882.

Kehr, Die Praxis der Volksschule. 10th ed. *Gotha.*
Keller, Geschichte des preussischen Volksschulwesens. *Berlin*, 1873.
Kellner, Volksschulkunde. 6th ed. *Essen.*
*Leutz, Lehrbuch der Erziehung und des Unterrichts. 2d ed. *Tauberbischofsheim*, 1887.
Lüben-Dittes, Jahresbericht; since 1848. *Leipzig.*
Ostermann-Wegener, Lehrbuch der Pädagogik. 2d ed. *Oldenburg*, 1886.
*Ranitzsch, Der Unterricht in der Volksschule. *Weimar*, 1888.
Schneider, Volksschulewesen und Lehrerbildung in Preussen. *Berlin*, 1875.
Schneider und v. Bremen, Das Volksschulwesen im Preuss. Staate. Gesetze und Verordnungen. *Berlin*, 1886.
Schumann, Lehrbuch der Pädagogik. 5th ed. *Hanover.*
Zerrenner, Grundsätze der Schulerziehung. 2d ed. *Magdeburg*, 1833.

(*b*) *The Middle Schools* (*Burgher and Real-Schools*).

Bartholomäus, Die Mittelschule. *Gotha*, 1887.
Dillmann, Das Realgymnasium. *Stuttgart*, 1884.
*Dörpfeld, Der Mittelstand und die Mittelschule. *Barmen*, 1853.
Hofmann, Ueber die Einrichtung öffentlicher Mittelschulen in Berlin. *Berlin*, 1869.
*Mager, Die deutsche Bürgerschule 1840. Ed. by Eberhardt. *Langensalza.*
Ostendorf, Volksschule, Bürgerschule und höhere Schule. *Düsseldorf*, 1872.
*Otto, Der deutsche Bürgerstand und die deutsche Bürgerschule. *Leipzig*, 1871.
Pädagogisches Archiv; since 1858. *Stettin.*
Richter, Das höhere bürgerliche Schulwesen in seiner geschichtlichen Entwidlung. 5th No. Schriften d. d. Einheitsschulvereins. *Hanover*, 1889.
Scheibert, Das Wesen und die Stellung der höh. Bürgerschule. *Berlin*, 1848.
Spilleke, Gesammelte Schulschriften. *Berlin*, 1825.
Vogel, Ueber die Idee und die Einrichtung einer höh. Bürger-oder Realschule. 2d ed. *Leipzig*, 1839.
*G. Wiget, Theorie und Praxis des Realschulunterrichts. *St. Gallen*, 1889.
Zeitschrift für Realschulwesen; since 1876. *Vienna.*
Zentralorgan für die Interessen des Realschulwesens; since 1872. *Berlin.*

(*c*) *Gymnasium.*

Döderlein, Reden und Aufsätze. 4 vols. *Erlangen*, 1843-59.
*Frick-Meier, Lehrproben und Lehrgänge. *Halle.*
Hirzel, Vorlesungen über Gymnasialpädagogik. *Tübingen*, 1876.
Jahn-Fleckeisen, Jahrbücher für Philologie und Pädagogik. *Leipzig.*
Kapp, Fragmente aus einer neuen Bearbeitung der Gymnasialpädagogik. *Arnsberg*, 1848.
*Kern-H. J. Müller, Zeitschrift für das Gymnasialwesen. *Berlin.*

Nägelsbach, Gymnasialpädagogik. *Erlangen*, 1862.
Reinhardt, Die Frankfurter Lehrpläne. *Frankfurt*, 1892.
Rethwisch, Jahresberichte über das höhere Schulwesen. *Berlin*.
Römer, Blätter für das Bayerische Gymnasialwesen. *Munich*.
Rönne, Das Unterichtswesen des preussischen Staates. 2 vols. *Berlin*, 1855.
Roth, Gymnasialpädagogik. *Stuttgart*, 1865.
*Schiller, Handbuch der prakt. Pädagogik. 2d ed. *Leipzig*, 1889.
Schmidt, Gymnasialpädagogik. *Köthen*, 1857.
Schrader, Erziehungs-und Unterrichtslehre. 2d ed. *Berlin*, 1873.
Thanlow, Die Gymnasialpädagogik im Grundriss. *Kiel*, 1858.
Uhlig, Gymnasium. *Heidelberg*.
Wiese, Das höhere Schulwesen in Preussen. 3 vols. *Berlin*, 1864-74.
Wiese, Verordnungen und Gesetze. 3d ed. 1886-88.
Fr. A. Wolf, Consilia scholastica. By Körte. *Quedlinburg und Leipzig*, 1835.
Zentralblatt für die ges. Unterrichtsverwaltung in Preussen; since 1859.

(d) Girls' Schools.

Buchner, Töchterschule oder Fachschule. *Berlin*, 1873.
Buchner, Gegenwart und Zukunft der höh. Mädchenschule: Pädagog. Studien of Rein. 3d No. *Vienna*, 1876; Grenzboten, 1891.
*H. Grosse, Zur Reform des höh. Mädchenschulwesens, in: Richter, Der prakt. Schulmann, vol. 37, 1888. *Leipzig*.
Hessel-Dörr, Die Mädchenschule. Zeitschrift für das gesamte Mädchenschulwesen; since 1888. *Bonn*.
*Krusche, Uebersicht der Litteratur über weibliche Erziehung und Bildung in Deutschland von 1700-1886. *Leipzig*, 1887.
Nöldecke, Von Weimar bis Berlin. *Leipzig*, 1886.
Schornstein-Buchner, Zeitschrift für weibl. Bildung; since 1873. *Leipzig*.

(B) School Administration.

1. School Legislation.

*Barth, Die Reform der Gesellchaft durch Neubelebung des Gemeindewesens. *Leipzig*, 1885.
*Dörpfeld, Die freie Schulgemeinde und ihre Anstalten auf dem Boden der freien Kirche im freien Staate. *Gütersloh*, 1863.
*Dörpfeld, Die drei Grundgebrechen der hergebrachten Schulverfassungen, etc. *Elberfeld*, 1869.
*Dörpfeld, Ein Beitrag der Leidensgeschichte der Volksschule nebst Vorschlägen zur Reform der Schulverwaltung. 2d ed. *Barmen*, 1883.
*Dörpfeld, Das Fundamentstück einer gerechten, gesunden, freien und friedlichen Schulverfassung. *Hilchenbach*, 1892.
Fichte, Reden an die deutsche Nation.
    (Ed. by Prof. Vogt, *Langensalza*.)
*Herbart, Ueber Erziehung unter öffentlicher Mitwirkung. 1810.
W. v. Humboldt, Ueber öffentliche Staatserziehung.

Katzer, Die Trennung der Schule von der Kirche nach ihren Prinzipien beurteilt. *Pirna*, 1872.
Lorenz v. Stein. Verwaltungslehre. 5 vols. *Stuttgart.*
*Mager, Pädagog. Revue. VI.—XVII. Band; XIX. Band.
    (Bruchstücke aus einer deutschen Scholastik.)
*Mager, Die deutsche Bürgerschule.
    (Ed. by Eberhardt, *Langensalza*.)
*Rein, Zur Schulgesetzgebung. Deutsche Rundschau. April No. 1892. (Comp. Grenzboten: Erziehung und Sozialismus. No. 24, 1891.)
*Rolle, Die Selbständigkeit der Schule inmitten von Staat und Kirche: Pädag. Studien of Rein, 1889. No. 4.
Schleiermacher, Ueber den Beruf des Staates zur Erziehung.
    (Verhandlungen der Berliner Akademie, 1814.)
Schrader, Die Verfassung der höh. Schulen. 3d ed. *Berlin*, 1889.
Schwarz, Die Schulen. *Leipzig*, 1832.
*Trüper, Die Familienrechte an der öffentlichen Erziehung. 2d ed. *Langensalza*, 1892.
*Trüper, Die Schule und die sozialen Fragen unserer Zeit. 3 Nos. *Gütersloh*, 1890.

2. Equipment of Schools.

Baginsky, Schulhygiene. 2d ed. *Stuttgart*, 1883.
Cohn, Hygiene des Auges. *Vienna*, 1883.
Gärtner, Leitfaden der Hygiene. *Berlin*, 1892.
Heine, Ueber Anschauungsmittel. *Berlin*, 1882.
Jütting, Geschichte des Rückschritts in der Dotation. der preuss. Volksschule. *Leipzig*, 1870.
Jütting, Die ungenügende Besoldung der preuss. Volksschullehrer. *Berlin*, 1889.
Köpp, Illustr. Hand und Nachschlagebuch der vorzüglichsten Lehr- und Veranschaulichungsmittel. *Bensheim.*
*Piltz, Thüring. Schulmuseum. *Jena.*
Schröder, Lehrmittelkatalog. *Leipzig.*
Zwez, Das Schulhaus und dessen innere Einrichtung. 2d ed. *Weimar.*

3. Supervision of Schools.

*Dörpfeld, Leidensgeschichte der Volksschule. 2d ed. *Barmen*, 1882.
Pollack, Die Schulaufsicht. *Leipzig*, 1888.
Zillessen, Nochmals die Schulaufsichtsfrage. *Gütersloh*, 1886.

4. Preparation of Teachers.

(a) *Seminaries for Teachers in the People's Schools.*

See the exhaustive literary references in Niemeyer's Grundsätze der Erziehung und des Unterrichts. Ed. of Rein. *Langensalza*, 3d vol., p. 92.

*Andreä, Zur inneren Entwicklungsgeschichte der deutschen Lehrerbildungsanstalten. *Kaiserslautern*, 1890-91 to 1891-92.
Kaufmann-Hartenstein, Zur Lehrerbildungsfrage. *Solothurn*, 1889.
Kehr-Schöppa, Pädagogische Blätter für Lehrerbildung und Lehrerbildungsanstalten; since 1872. *Gotha*.
*Rein, Ueber die Organisation der Lehrerbildung in Deutschland. Pädagog. Studien, 1881. 4th No. *Dresden*.
*Stoy, Organisation des Lehrerseminars. *Leipzig*, 1869.
Schneider, Volksschullehrer-Seminar. Schmid's Encyklopädie.

(b) *University-Seminaries.*

*Brzoska, Die Notwendigkeit pädagog. Seminare auf der Universität und ihre zweckmäszige Einrichtung. 2d ed. by Rein. *Leipzig*, 1887.
(For Bibliography v. p. 205 *sqq.*)
*Frick, Seminar. praeceptorum. *Halle*, 1883.
*Rein, Ueber pädagog. Universitäts-Seminare. Neue d. Schule, 4-5 Nos.
*Rein, Die Ausbildung für d. Lehramt an höher. Schulen. Grenzboten, 1890. 8th No.
*Rein, Aus dem Päd. Univers.-Seminare zu Jena. Nos. 1-4. *Langensalza*.
*Von Sallwürk, Das Staatsseminar. *Gotha*, 1890.
*Schiller, Pädagog. Seminarien f. d. höh. Lehramt. *Leipzig*, 1890.
*Vogt, Das pädagog. Universitäts-Seminar. *Leipzig*, 1884.
Voss, Vorbildung zum höheren Lehramt. *Halle*, 1889.
*Zange, Gymnasial-Seminare und die pädagog. Ausbildung der Kandidaten des höh. Schulamts. 5th No. by Frick-Meyer: Sammlung pädagog. Abhandlungen. *Halle*, 1890.

II. THEORETICAL PEDAGOGICS.

(A) THE FUNDAMENTAL SCIENCES OF PEDAGOGICS.

I. ETHICS.

*Flügel, Das Ich und die sittlichen Ideen im Leben der Völker. 2d ed. *Langensalza*.
*Flügel, Die Sittenlehre Jesu. 2d ed. *Langensalza*.
*Hartenstein, Die Grundbegriffe der eth. Wissensch. *Leipzig*, 1844.
*Herbart, Allgem. prakt. Philosophie. Ed. by Hartenstein, vol. 8; Gesamtausgabe, by Kehrbach, vol. 4. *Langensalza*.
*Nahlowsky, Praktische Philosophie. 2d ed. *Leipzig*. 1885.
Paulsen, System der Ethik. 2d ed. *Berlin*, 1891.
*Steinthal, Allgem. Ethik. *Berlin*, 1885.
Wundt, Ethik. *Leipzig*, 1886.
*Ziller, Allgem. philos. Ethik. 2d ed. *Langensalza*, 1886.

II. Psychology.

*Ballauff, Die Grundlehren der Psychologie. 2d ed. *Cöthen*, 1890.
*Dörpfeld, Denken und Gedächtnis. 3d ed. *Gütersloh*.
*Drobisch, Emp. Psychologie. *Leipzig*, 1843.
 Fechner, Revision der Hauptpunkte der Psychophysik. *Leipzig*, 1882.
*Flügel, Die Seelenfrage. 2d ed. *Cöthen*, 1884.
 Goltz, Buch der Kindheit. *Berlin*, 1847.
*Hartmann, Die Analyse des kindl. Gedankenkreises. *Annaberg*, 1885.
*Lange, Ueber Apperzeption. 4th ed. *Plauen.* See English References, page 198.
*Lazarus, Das Leben der Seele. 3d ed. *Berlin*.
 Lotze, Medizin. Psychologie. *Leipzig*, 1852.
*Lukens, Die Vorstellungsreihen u. ihre pädagog. Bedeutung. *Gütersloh*, 1892.
*Männel, Ueber Abstraktion. *Gütersloh*.
*Nahlowsky, Das Gefühlsleben. 2d ed. *Leipzig*, 1884.
 Preyer, Die Seele des Kindes. 3d ed. *Leipzig*. Translated by H. W. Brown. *See* Vol. vii., "The Senses and the Will," and Vol. ix, "The Development of the Intellect," in the International Edition Series, edited by Dr. W. T. Harris.
*Schoel, J. Fr., Herbarts philos. Lehre von der Religion. *Dresden*, 1884.
 Sigismund, Die Familie als Schule der Natur. *Leipzig*, 1857.
 Sigismund, Kind und Welt. *Braunschweig*, 1856.
*Strümpell, Gedanken über Religion u. relig. Probleme. *Leipzig*, 1888.
*Volkmann, Lehrbuch der Psychologie. 3d ed. *Cöthen*.
 Wundt, Grundzüge der physiol. Psychologie. 2d ed. *Leipzig*, 1880.
 Ziehen, Leitfaden der Physiologischen Psychologie. *Jena*, 1891. Translated by C. C. Van Liew and Dr. O. W. Beyer (*sub. tit.* Introduction to Physiological Psychology). *London:* Swan Sonnenschein & Co. 1892.

(B) Aid-Science of Pedagogics: Physiology.

Baginsky, Handbuch der Schulhygiene. 3d ed. *Stuttgart*, 1883.
Burgerstein, Gesundheitspflege. *Vienna*, 1887.
Dornblüth, Die Gesundheitspflege der Schuljugend. *Stuttgart*, 1892.
Gärtner, Leitfaden der Hygiene. *Berlin*, 1892.
Janke, Grundriss der Schulhygiene. *Hamburg*, 1890.
Klencke, Schuldiätetik. *Leipzig*, 1871.
Kotelmann, Zeitschrift für Gesundheitspflege. *Hamburg* and *Leipzig*.
Siegert, Die Schulkrankheiten. *Leipzig*, 1887.
Spencer, Education: Intellectual, Moral, and Physical. *London*, 1861. New ed. 1883.

LITERARY REFERENCES.

(*A*) TELEOLOGY (*see* ETHICS).

(*B*) METHODOLOGY (*see* PSYCHOLOGY).

I. GENERAL DIDACTICS.

*Dörpfeld, Der didakt. Materialismus. 2d ed. *Gütersloh.*
*Dörpfeld, Grundlinien einer Theorie des Lehrplans. *Gütersloh.*
*Willmann, Didaktik als Bildungslehre. 2 vols. *Brunswick*, 1889.
*Willmann, Pädagog. Vorträge. 2d ed. *Leipzig*, 1886.
*Ziller, Grundlegung zur Lehre vom erz. Unterricht. 2d ed. by Vogt. *Leipzig*, 1884.

1. AIMS OF INSTRUCTION.

*Grössler, Das vielseitige Interesse. *Eisleben*, 1883.
*Vieth, Darf vielseitiges Interesse als Unterrichtsziel hingestellt werden? *Koyasen*, 1886.
*Walsemann, Das Interesse. *Hanover*, 1884.

2. MEANS OF INSTRUCTION.

(a) *Choice of Material.*

*Rein, Gesinnungsunt. und Kulturgeschichte: Pädagog. Studien, 1888, 2d No. *Dresden.*
*v. Sallwürck, Gesinnungsunt. u. Kulturgeschichte. *Langensalza*, 1887.
Vaihinger, Naturforschung und Schule. *Leipzig*, 1889.
  (Bibliographies in the Notes.)

(b) *Connection of Branches.*

*Ackermann, Ueber Konzentration: Pädag Fragen, 1st series. *Dresden.*
*Dörpfeld, Zwei dringl. Reformen im Real und Sprachunt. *Gütersloh*, 1883.
*Loos, Der österr Gymnasiallehrplan im Lichte der Konzentration. *Vienna*, 1892.
*Merian-Genast, Ausführungen zum Lehrplan. *Jena*, 1892.
*Rein, Pickel, Scheller, Theorie u. Praxis. 1st vol. 4th ed. *Leipzig.*
Richter, Die Konzentration des Unterrichts. *Leipzig*, 1865.
*Willmann, Päd. Vorträge. 2d ed. *Leipzig.*

(c) *Treatment of Material.*

*Gleichmann, Ueber Herbart's Lehre von den formalen Stufen. 2d ed. *Langensalza*, 1892.
*Reich, Die Theorie der Formalstufen. *Langensalza*, 1889.

K. Richter, Die Herbart-Zillerschen formalen Stufen, etc. *Leipzig*, 1888.
*Th. Wiget, Die formalen Stufen. 4th ed. *Chur*, 1892.

II. SPECIAL DIDACTICS.

*Frick-Meier, Lehrproben und Lehrgänge. *Halle*.
*Jahrbücher des Vereins für w. Pädagogik. *Dresden*.
Kehr, Geschichte der Methodik. 4 vols. 2d ed. *Gotha*.
Nacke-Lüben-Dittes, Pädag. Jahresbericht. *Leipzig*.
*Rein, Pickel, Scheller, Theorie und Praxis des Volksschulunterrichts, etc. Vols. i.-viii. 4th ed. *Leipzig*.
Rethwisch, Jahresberichte über das höh. Schulwesen. *Berlin*.
*Schiller, Handbuch der prakt. Pädagogik. 2d ed. *Leipzig*.
*Ziller-Bergner, Materialien zur spez. Pädagogik. *Dresden*, 1886.

1. INSTRUCTION IN RELIGION.

*Dörpfeld, Ein christl.-pädag. Protest. *Gütersloh*, 1869.
Kirchner, Zur Reform des Relig.-Unterr. *Berlin*, 1877.
Landfermann, Der ev. Relig.-Unterr. in den Gymnasien. *Frankfurt*, 1846.
*Reukauf, Philos. Begründung des Lehrplans des ev. Rel.-Unt. an höh. Schulen. *Langensalza*, 1892.
Ritschl, Unt. in der christl. Religion. 2d ed. *Bonn*, 1881.
*Staude, Präparationen zu den bibl. Gesch. des alten und neuen Testaments. 3 vols., 5th ed. *Dresden*
*Thrändorf, Die Behandlung des Religionsunterrichts. *Langensalza*, 1887.
*Thrändorf, Kirchengeschichtl. Lesebuch. *Dresden*, 1888.
*Thrändorf, Der Religionsunterricht. (Präparationen.) *Dresden*, 1890.
Wiese, Der Religionsunterr. an höh. Lehranstalten. 1890.
Zeitschrift für den Religionsunterricht. *Berlin*.

2. HISTORY.

Biedermann, Der Geschichtsunt. in der Schule. *Brunswick*, 1890.
Biedermann, Der Gesch.-Unt. *Biesbaden*, 1885.
Campe, Geschichte und Unt. in der Geschichte. *Leipzig*, 1859.
*Dörpfeld, Repetitorium der Gesellschaftskunde und Begleitwort. 2d ed. *Gütersloh*, 1890.
*Eberhard, Ueber Gesch.-Unt. Pädag. Studien. 4th No. *Vienna*.
Herbst, Zur Frage über den Geschichts-Unt. *Maintz*, 1869, and *Maintz*, 1877.
Jäger, Bemerkungen über geschichtl. Unt. 2d ed. *Maintz*, 1882.
Löbell, Grundzüge einer Methodik des geschichtl. Unt. *Leipzig*, 1847.
Miquél, Beiträge, etc. *Aurich* and *Leers*, 1847.
Peter, Der Geschichtsunt. auf Gymnasien. *Halle*, 1849.
Richter, Die Kulturgeschichte. *Gotha*, 1887.

*Staude-Göpfert, Präparationen zur deutschen Geschichte. *Dresden,* 1890.
*Willmann, Der elem. Gesch.-Unt. *Leipzig,* 1872.
*Wohlrabe, Präparationen zu profangesch. Quellenstoffen. *Gotha,* 1887.
*Zillig, Der Geschichtsunt. XIV. Jahrbuch d. Vereins f. w. Pädagogik.

3. Drawing.

Flinzer, Lehrbuch des Zeichenunterrichts. 3d ed. *Leipzig,* 1882.
*Menard, Der Zeichenunterricht. *Neuwied.*
*Otto-Rein, Pädagog. Zeichenlehre. 3d ed. *Weimar,* 1885.
*Rein, Geschichte des Zeichenunt. 2d ed. *Gotha,* 1889.
*Rein, Der Zeichenunterricht im Gymnasium. *Hanover,* 1889.
Stuhlmann, Der Zeichenunterricht. *Hamburg.*

4. Singing.

*Helm, Gesangunterricht in "Theorie und Praxis." Vols. I—VIII. *Leipzig.*

5. Instruction in Language.

*Mager, Die genet. Methode des schulmässigen Unterrichts in fremden Sprachen und Litteraturen. 3d ed. *Zürich,* 1846.
*Mager, Moderne Humanitätsstudien. 3 Nos. *Zürich.*

(a) *German.*

*Bliedner, Schillerlesebuch. *Dresden.*
*Eberhardt, Die Poesie in der Volksschule. 3 vols., 3d ed. *Langensalza,* 1886.
Hiecke, Der deutsche Unt. auf deutschen Gymnasien. *Leipzig,* 1842.
Hildebrand, Vom deutschen Sprachunt. 4th ed. *Leipzig,* 1890.
Laas, Der deutsche Unterr. auf höh. Lehranstalten. *Berlin,* 1872.
Lehmann, Der deutsche Unt. *Berlin,* 1890.
Linde, Die Muttersprache im Elementarunt. *Leipzig,* 1892.
Lyon, Zeitschrift für den deutschen Unterricht. *Leipzig.*
*Stoy, Der deutsche Sprachunt. 3d ed. *Vienna,* 1868.

(b) *Other Foreign Languages.*

*Bätgen, Zur Neugestaltung des französ. Unt. *Eisenach,* 1886.
*Günther, Der Lateinunt. XIII. Jahrbuch d. V. f. w. Päd. *Dresden.*
Hoffmann, Neugestaltnng des griech. Unterrichts. *Göttingen,* 1889.
Perthes, Zur Reform des latein. Unterrichts. *Berlin,* 1875.
v. Roden, Inwiefern muss der Sprachunterricht umkehren? *Marburg,* 1890.
Victor, Phonetische Studien. *Marburg.*
Victor, Quousque Tandem. Der Sprachunterricht muss umkehren.

6. Geography.

Finger, Heimatkunde. 4th ed. *Berlin*, 1876.
*Heiland, Das geographische Zeichnen. *Dresden*, 1887.
Lehmann, Das Kartenzeichnen im geogr. Unt. *Halle*, 1891.
Lehmann, Vorlesungen über Hilssmittel u. Methode des geogr. Unt. *Halle.*
*Matzat, Methodik des geogr. Unt. *Berlin*, 1886.
Seibert, Zeitschrift für Schulgeographie.

7. Natural Sciences.

*Beyer, Die Naturwissenschaften in der Erziehungsschule. *Leipzig*, 1885.
*Conrad, Präparationen f. d. Physik-Unterricht. *Dresden*, 1889.
*Dörpfeld, Repetitor. d. naturkundl u. humanist. Unt. 3d ed. *Gütersloh.*
Junge, Naturgeschichte. Vol. 1., 2d ed., 1891. Vol. II., 1891. *Kiel* and *Liepzig.*
Poske, Zeitschrift für chem. und physikal. Unt.
*Schleichert, Anleitg. zu botan. Beobachtungen, etc. *Langensalza*, 1891.
Zopf, Der naturwissenschaftl. Unt. auf Gymnasien. *Breslau*, 1887.

8. Mathematics.

*Falke, Propädeutik der Geometrie. *Leipzig*, 1869.
*Fresenius, Die psycholog. Grundlagen der Raumwissenschaft. *Wiesbaden*, 1868.
*Fresenius, Raumlehre. *Frankfurt*, 1861.
*Hartmann, Handbuch des Rechenunterrichts. *Hildburghausen*, 1889.
Hoffmann, Zeitschrift f. d. mathemat. Unterricht. *Leipzig.*
*Pickel, Die Geometrie der Volksschule. 16th ed. *Dresden.*
Schellbach, Inhalt und Bedeutung des mathem. u. physik. Unt. auf unsern Gymnasien. *Berlin*, 1887.
Wittstein, Die Methode des mathemat. Unt. *Hanover*, 1879.

9. Manual Training.

*Barth-Niederley, Des d. Knaben Handwerkbuch. 5th ed. *Leipzig*, 1882.
*Barth-Niederley, Die Schülerwerkstatt. *Leipzig*, 1882.
Rissmann, Geschichte des Handfertigkeitsunt. in Deutschland. *Gotha*, 1882.
v. Schenkendorff, Verein für Knabenhandarbeit. *Görlitz.*
Schwab, Der Schulgarten. 4th ed. 1876.

10. Turning.

Eitner, Jugendspiele. *Görlitz.*
Euler, Geschichte des Turnunt. *Gotha.*

Euler-Eckler, Monatsschrift für das Turnwesen; since 1882. *Berlin.*
*Hausmann, Das Turnen in der Volkschule. 4th ed. *Weimar.*
Kupfermann, Turnunterricht und Jugendspiele. *Breslau,* 1884.
v. Schenkendorff u. Schmidt, Ueber Jugend-u. Volkspiele. *Hanover-Linden,* 1892.

THEORY OF GUIDANCE.

1. TRAINING.

Bach, Wanderungen, Turnfahrten, Schülerreisen. 2d ed.
*Barth, Ueber den Umgang. 3d ed. *Langensalza.*
*Kindergottesdienst, Ev. Schulbl. von Dörpfeld, 1887 u. 1888; Erziehungsschule von Barth. II., 9.
Fr. Scholz, Die Charakterfehler des Kindes. *Leipzig,* 1891.
*Scholz, Schulreisen. Aus dem pädagog. Universitäts-Seminar. 3d No. *Langensalza,* 1890.
Schubert, Ueber Schulfeiern. *Langensalza,* 1892.
Siegert, Problematische Kindesnaturen. *Kreuznach* and *Leipzig,* 1889.
*Strümpell, Die pädag. Pathologie. *Leipzig,* 1890.

2. GOVERNMENT OF CHILDREN.

Emminghaus, Die physischen Störungen des Kindesalters. *Tübingen,* 1887.
*Nahlowsky, Ueber Herbarts reformator. Beruf. Zeitschrift f. exakte Philosophie, VII., 391-97.
*Rein, Regierung, Unterricht u. Zucht. Pädag. Studien. 1st No., 3d ed. *Vienna.*
*Stoy, Haus- und Schulpolizei. *Berlin,* 1856.
*Ziller, Regierung der Kinder. *Leipzig,* 1857.

THE ENGLISH LITERATURE ON THE HERBARTIAN SYSTEM.

THE following references contain the majority of what has been written in English upon the subject of the Herbartian pedagogics. No attempt has been made to refer to works outside of this field, as do the literary references in the original. The English-speaking pedagog will, of course, have a more or less thorough acquaintance with the already extensive English literature on the subject of Pedagogy in general. He has but to refer to such sources as the *Bibliography of Education (Boston, 1886),* by G. S. Hall and J. M. Mansfield, and the "Bibliography of Pedagogy" in Sonnenschein's *Cyclopedia of Education* (Third ed. 1892), to obtain the most comprehensive and accurate directions to the literature of every possible department of education, or to Dr. W. T. Harris's *Teachers' Course of Professional Reading for Home Work and Reading Circles*, for a general, profitable course of reading. The following list will be of service to those who desire to become more familiar with the rising Herbartian views:—

Brown, G. P.: What is Interest? in *Public School Journal*, vol. xii., No. 1., *Bloomington, Ill.*

De Garmo, Dr. Charles: Essentials of Method, *Boston*, 1889; Ethical Training in the Public Schools; Am. Academy of Pol. and Soc. Science, publication No. 49, *Philadelphia*; Language Work below the High Schools, *Bloomington, Ill.*, since 1887; The Herbartian System of Pedagogics, in the *Educational Review*, *New York*, vol. i., Nos. 1, 3, and 5; The Relation of Instruction to Will Training, in the publications of the Am. Nat. Ed. Assoc., 1890; What does Apperception Mean? in the *Public School Journal*, vol. x., No. 11, 1891, *Bloomington, Ill.*; A Popular View of Apperception, *Public School Journal*, vol. xii., No. 3, *Bloomington, Ill.*; Co-ordination of Studies, *Ed. Rev.*, vol. iv., No. 5; The Educational Value of Natural Science in Elementary Schools, in *Ed. Papers by Ill. Science Teachers*, i., 1889-90.

Donaldson: Lectures on the History of Education in Prussia and England, *Edinburgh*, 1874, mentions Ziller's work briefly and favourably.

Douglas, C. H.: Certain Views of Herbart on Mathematics and Natural Science, *Ed. Review*, vol. iii., No. 5.

Findlay, J. J.: Herbartian Literature in English, *School and College*, October and November, 1892.

Hall, Dr. H.: Notes of the German Schools, contains references to Herbart.

Harris, Dr. W. T.: Apperception Defined, and Apperception *versus* Perception, in the *Public School Journal*, vol xi., Nos. 2 and 5.

Herbart: The Science of Education, and The Æsthetic Revelation of the World, translated by Henry M. and Emmie Felkin —Swan Sonnenschein & Co., *London*, 1892.

Herbart: Psychology, translated by Miss M. K. Smith, International Ed. Series, *New York*, 1891.

Klemm, L. R.: European Schools, mentions the Herbartian Pedagogics, and gives some criticism, International Ed. Series, *New York*.

Lange: Ueber Apperception, translated by the Herbart Club in America, *Boston*, 1892.

Lindner: Empirical Psychology, translated by Dr Charles De Garmo, *New York*, 1890.

Lukens, Dr. H. T.: Herbart's Psychological Basis of Teaching, Part II. of Th. B. Noss's Outlines of Psychology and Pedagogy, *Pittsburg*, 1890.

McMurry, Dr. Charles A.: The Elements of General Method based on the Principles of Herbart, *Bloomington, Ill.*, 1892; A Geography Plan for the Grades of the Common Schools, and Pioneer History Stories for the 3rd and 4th Grade, *Winona, Minn.*, 1891; How to Conduct the Recitation, Teachers' Manuals, No. 13, *New York* and *Chicago.*

McMurry, Dr. Frank: The Moral Value of Fairy Tales and Imaginative Literature for Children, in *Public School Journal, Bloomington, Ill.*, vol. x., No. 11, and vol. xi., No. 3; Relation of Sciences to the other Studies, in *Ed. Papers* by *Ill. Science Teachers,* i., 1889-90, *Peoria. Ill.;* Value of Herb. Ped. for Normal Schools in *Proceedings of Nat. Ed. Assoc.* for 1892.

Prince, J. P.: Methods in German Schools, mentions the Herbartian Pedagogics briefly, and gives some criticism.

Ribot, T.: German Psychology of To-day, contains a digest of Herbart's psychology, *New York*, 1880.

Salmon, Lucy M.: The Teaching of History in the Elementary Schools, *Ed. Review, New York*, vol. i., No. 5, contains brief reference to the principles of the historical stages of culture and concentration.

Smith, Margaret K.: Herbart's Life, three articles in the *New England Journal of Education*, 1889.

Van View, C. C.: Life of Herbart and Development of his Pedagogical Doctrines—Swan Sonnenschein & Co., *London*, 1893.

Ward: Article in the *Encyclopædia Britannica* on Herbart, important psychologically.

A number of other articles and reviews might be mentioned that refer to Herbart's works or to Herbartian ideas. As yet Herbart is poorly represented in English Histories of Pedagogics.

www.ingramcontent.com/pod-product-compliance
Lightning Source LLC
Chambersburg PA
CBHW020857230426
43666CB00008B/1212